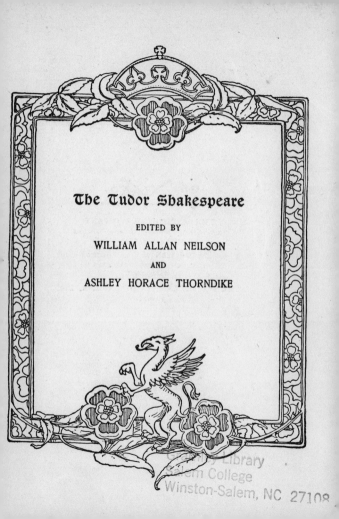

The Tudor Shakespeare

EDITED BY

WILLIAM ALLAN NEILSON

AND

ASHLEY HORACE THORNDIKE

THE MACMILLAN COMPANY
NEW YORK · BOSTON · CHICAGO · DALLAS
ATLANTA · SAN FRANCISCO

MACMILLAN & CO., Limited
LONDON · BOMBAY · CALCUTTA
MELBOURNE

THE MACMILLAN CO. OF CANADA, Ltd.
TORONTO

The Tudor Shakespeare will be published in forty volumes, including all of the plays and poems. It is under the general editorship of WILLIAM ALLAN NEILSON, Ph.D., of Harvard University, and ASHLEY HORACE THORNDIKE, Ph.D., L.H.D., of Columbia University. The following volumes, each under the special editorship of an American scholar, are now ready or in preparation.

Already Published

Romeo and Juliet — The GENERAL EDITORS.

A Midsummer-Night's Dream — JOHN W. CUNLIFFE, D.Lit., Professor of English, University of Wisconsin.

Macbeth — ARTHUR C. L. BROWN, Ph.D., Professor of English, Northwestern University.

Henry IV, Part I — FRANK W. CHANDLER, Ph.D., Professor of English and Comparative Literature, University of Cincinnati.

Troilus and Cressida — JOHN S. P. TATLOCK, Ph.D., Professor of English, University of Michigan.

Henry V — LEWIS F. MOTT, Ph.D., Professor of English, College of the City of New York.

The Merchant of Venice — HARRY M. AYRES, Ph.D., Assistant Professor of English, Columbia University.

As You Like It — MARTHA H. SHACKFORD, Ph.D., Associate Professor of English Literature, Wellesley College.

Coriolanus — STUART P. SHERMAN, Ph.D., Professor of English, University of Illinois.

Henry VI, Part I — LOUISE POUND, Ph.D., Assistant Professor of English, University of Nebraska.

Henry VIII — CHARLES G. DUNLAP, Litt.D., Professor of English Literature, University of Kansas.

Comedy of Errors — FREDERICK MORGAN PADELFORD, Ph.D., Professor of English, University of Washington.

King John — HENRY M. BELDEN, Ph.D., Professor of English, University of Missouri.

King Lear — VIRGINIA C. GILDERSLEEVE, Ph.D., Dean of Barnard College.

Much Ado about Nothing — WILLIAM W. LAWRENCE, Ph.D., Associate Professor of English, Columbia University.

Love's Labour's Lost — JAMES F. ROYSTER, Ph.D., Professor of English, University of North Carolina.

Henry IV, Part II — ELIZABETH DEERING HANSCOM, Ph.D., Professor of English, Smith College.

Richard III — GEORGE B. CHURCHILL, Ph.D., Professor of English, Amherst College.

The Winter's Tale — LAURA J. WYLIE, Ph.D., Professor of English, Vassar College.

Othello — THOMAS M. PARROTT, Ph.D., Professor of English, Princeton University.

The Two Gentlemen of Verona — MARTIN W. SAMPSON, A.M., Goldwin Smith Professor of English Literature, Cornell University.

All's Well that Ends Well — JOHN L. LOWES, Ph.D., Professor of English, Washington University, St. Louis.

Richard II — HARDIN CRAIG, Ph.D., Professor of English, University of Minnesota.

Measure for Measure — EDGAR C. MORRIS, A.M., Professor of English, Syracuse University.

Twelfth Night — WALTER MORRIS HART, Ph.D., Associate Professor of English, University of California.

The Taming of the Shrew — FREDERICK TUPPER, Jr., Ph.D., Professor of English, University of Vermont.

Julius Cæsar — ROBERT M. LOVETT, A.B., Professor of English, University of Chicago.

Timon of Athens — ROBERT HUNTINGTON FLETCHER, Ph.D., Professor of English Literature, Grinnell College, Iowa.

Venus and Adonis, and Lucrece — CARLETON BROWN, Ph.D., Professor of English, Bryn Mawr College.

Henry VI, Part III — ROBERT ADGER LAW, Ph.D., Adjunct Professor of English, the University of Texas.

Cymbeline — WILL D. HOWE, Ph.D., Professor of English, Indiana University.

Merry Wives of Windsor — FRED P. EMERY, A.M., Professor of English, Dartmouth College.

Titus Andronicus — ELMER E. STOLL, Ph.D.

Pericles — C. ALPHONSO SMITH, Ph.D., Edgar Allan Poe Professor of English, University of Virginia.

The Sonnets — RAYMOND M. ALDEN, Ph.D., Professor of English, University of Illinois.

Hamlet — GEORGE PIERCE BAKER, A.B., Professor of Dramatic Literature, Harvard University.

Henry VI, Part II — CHARLES H. BARNWELL, Ph.D., Professor of English, University of Alabama.

The Tempest — HERBERT E. GREENE, Ph.D., Professor of English, Johns Hopkins University.

Antony and Cleopatra — GEORGE WYLLYS BENEDICT, Ph.D., Associate Professor of English, Brown University.

The Facts about Shakespeare — THE GENERAL EDITORS.
A handbook for readers and students of Shakespeare.
This volume is sold only to complete the set.

SHAKESPEARE'S DEATH MASK

From " Shakespeare's Totenmaske," by Paul Wislicenus
Eugen Diederichs, Jena

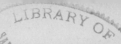

THE TUDOR SHAKESPEARE

The Tempest

EDITED BY

HERBERT E. GREENE, Ph.D.

COLLEGIATE PROFESSOR OF ENGLISH IN
JOHNS HOPKINS UNIVERSITY

New York
The Macmillan Company
1916

All rights reserved

The Text used is the Neilson Text copyrighted in 1906
by William Allan Neilson

Introduction

Text. — *The Tempest* was first published in the First Folio (1623), in which the play was divided into acts and scenes. All later editions are based upon that text, with modernized spelling and punctuation. The text is unusually good; few of the difficulties in interpretation are due to a doubtful text.

Date of Composition. — The First Folio opens with *The Tempest*, perhaps because of its recent popularity. Since many modern editions follow the order of the Folio, many readers have supposed *The Tempest* to be the earliest of Shakespeare's plays. As a matter of fact, it is one of the latest. Its diction, compressed and weighted with meaning, and its syntax, sometimes loose, sometimes involved, are indications of a late date. The verse, too, — unrimed, with frequent overflow, frequent run-on lines, frequent midstopt speeches, and numerous light and weak endings, — has the freedom and ease that characterize Shakespeare's latest plays. This freedom sometimes passes into carelessness.

On June 2, 1609, a fleet of nine vessels set sail from Plymouth, carrying settlers and provisions for the new colony in Virginia. This fleet was scattered by a storm on July 25, and on July 28 the *Sea Venture*, in which were the three leaders, Sir George Somers, Sir Thomas Gates, and Captain Christopher Newport, was cast ashore on one

R652

of the Bermudas (for a time known as the Somers
Islands), but without loss of life. There the adventurers
lived in comparative comfort for nine or ten months.
Two pinnaces were built, in part from materials supplied
by the wreck, and on May 10, 1610, the shipwrecked
colonists sailed for Virginia, where they rejoined their
companions, who, but for the loss of one ship, had arrived
there in safety. Much anxiety had been felt in England
for Sir George Somers and his companions, who were
supposed to be lost. Two pamphlets had appeared (in
January and February), giving an account of the scattering
of the fleet; and in October, 1610, Silvester Jourdan, who
had been in the same ship with Sir George Somers, published in London a pamphlet entitled *A Discovery of the
Bermudas, otherwise called the Isle of Divels*, etc. William
Strachey, Esquire, also shipwrecked in the *Sea Venture*,
wrote *A true reportory of the wracke, and redemption
of Sir* THOMAS GATES *Knight; upon, and from the Ilands
of the Bermudas:* etc., dated 15th July, 1610. This was the
date on which Sir Thomas Gates returned to England
taking also a *Despatch* (July 7) from Lord De la Warr,
governor of Virginia. Strachey's *Reportory* was first
printed in *Purchas his Pilgrimes* (1625). Shakespeare
may have seen the original manuscript,— Mr. Luce asserts
(p. 154) that he " must surely have seen it," — perhaps
while it was in the keeping of Hakluyt, who transmitted it to
Purchas. Toward the end of 1610 there was published in
London *A True Declaration of the Estate of the Colonie
in Virginia*, etc. It may have been written by William
Strachey, inasmuch as it is based upon the *Despatch*
from Lord Delaware. " His name is among the signatures

(as secretary), and the document is in his handwriting "
(Luce, p. 153). Thus there were three accounts in existence,
two of them in print, before the end of 1610. Close cor-
respondences, both in incidents and in the wording of
certain speeches, — for which see Notes, — show that
Shakespeare had read these pamphlets and drawn from
them hints for the storm and the shipwreck on an island
supposed to be enchanted and to be uninhabited save by
evil spirits.

Shakespeare's use of these pamphlets fixes the date of
the play as not earlier than 1610. A misdating of Strachey's
MS. as 1612 instead of 1610, and two pamphlets published by him in 1612, have been taken as evidence that
the play was as late as 1612, 613. According to Vertue's
MS., *The Tempest* was one of fourteen (actually thirteen)
plays performed at Court during the festivities that followed the marriage, on February 14, 1613, of the Princess
Elizabeth and Frederick, Elector Palatine. None of the
other plays acted on the occasion was new; but some
editors have held that *The Tempest* was written for
this occasion and have seen in Elizabeth the island
princess wooed by a prince from a distant land, in Prospero
the learned King James, and in the supposed loss of
Ferdinand, a reference to the recent death of Prince
Henry.

It is now possible to cite with more confidence than
hitherto evidence that dates from 1611, — evidence that
has more than once been lost and found, accepted and
rejected. In 1808 Edmond Malone printed privately

eighty copies of *An Account of the Incidents from which the Title and part of the Story of Shakespeare's Tempest were derived*, etc. In this essay he wrote, " I know that it had 'a being and a name' in the autumn of 1611." His evidence was not forthcoming until the publication in 1842 for the Shakespeare Society of *Extracts from the Accounts of the Revels at Court in the reigns of Queen Elizabeth and James I., from the Original Office Books of the Masters and Yeomen.* This book was edited by Peter Cunningham, son of the poet, Allan Cunningham, and treasurer of the Society. On page 210 is an entry to the effect that on November 1, 1611, " By the Kings Players : Hallomas nyght was presented att Whithall before the Kinges Majestie a play called the Tempest." The records had been mislaid, and had been found by Peter Cunningham, in 1838, " under the vaults of Somerset House." They were accepted as genuine until 1868, when they were supposedly proved to have been forged by the editor. Recently, however, the stigma of forgery has been removed from his name, and it is now permissible to cite the record as evidence.[1] Even while they were supposed to be forgeries, many scholars believed that they were based upon information that was trustworthy. Thus we are enabled to repeat with confidence the statement of Malone, in 1808, that " the date of the play is fixed and ascertained with uncommon precision, between the end of the year 1610 and the Autumn of 1611; and it may with great probability be ascribed to the Spring of the latter year."

[1] See *Some Supposed Shakespeare Forgeries.* Ernest Law, London, 1911.

Source of the Plot. — No indubitable source of *The Tempest* is known, — a statement that can be made in regard to only one or two other plays by Shakespeare. Long and careful search for sources has resulted in the discovery of two analogues, one a Spanish tale, the other a German play. In 1885, again in 1902, and more fully in 1907, attention was called to a collection of stories, *Winter Nights*, by Antonio de Eslava; this collection was published at Pamplona and at Barcelona in 1609, at Brussels in 1610. These somewhat elaborately-wrought tales were translated (with omissions) into German as early as 1666. There follows a brief summary of a recent translation of the fourth of these tales by Gustav Becker (Shakespeare *Jahrbuch*, XLIII).

Good King Dardano, of Bulgaria, though he had magic power, was dispossessed of his kingdom by Niciphoro, the proud emperor of Greece. Accompanied by his daughter Serafina, King Dardano guided a well-built ship into the middle of the Adriatic Sea. There he struck with his wand the water, which parted and let the ship down to the bottom of the sea, where a marvelous and richly-adorned palace received them. After they have lived for two years in this magic palace, Serafina reminds her father that all created beings feel the promptings of love, and asks him to provide for her a companion of her own rank and age. Meantime the haughty emperor Niciphoro had died, after disinheriting his gentle, older son, Valentiniano, and leaving his power to his younger son, Juliano. In his wanderings in search of help the disinherited prince came to the Adriatic Sea, where he

found a little boat, guided by a frail old man who invited
him to come on board. This aged pilot was King Dardano,
who again struck the sea with his magic wand, so that they
sank into the magic palace. As soon as he saw the
Infanta Serafina, Prince Valentiniano rejoiced at his good
fortune, and entreated the old man to give him Serafina
as wife. By magic art the royal wedding is celebrated,
and is attended by many princes and kings with their fair
ladies who dwell in all the islands of the ocean.

Just at this time Juliano, the new emperor of Greece
and Bulgaria, was returning from Rome, where he had
married the daughter of the emperor. As his fleet came
over the magic palace where King Dardano was celebrat-
ing the wedding of his daughter, a tremendous storm
arose, and destroyed all of the ships except the four which
were carrying the Emperor Juliano and his wife and their
attendants. By his magic power King Dardano rises
above the waves, and sternly rebukes the haughty emperor. Soon after reaching home the emperor died, and,
shortly after, his bride. The great men of Greece unani-
mously agreed to search far and wide for Prince Valentiniano, and to offer him the power that justly belonged to
him. King Dardano destroyed his magic palace, and
sailed with his daughter and his son-in-law for Greece,
where they were received with joy. Valentiniano and
Serafino reigned for thirty-two years, twice as long as
his father had ruled as a tyrant. Old King Dardano
relinquished his kingdom in favor of his son-in-law;
and, to fulfill his oath that he would dwell no more on
dry land, he caused to be built upon five ships a suitable

palace, connecting with the royal palace of his son-in-law. Thus he lived for two years, and left the reputation of a just and peace-loving prince.

This tale can hardly be the immediate source of *The Tempest*. There is no reason for supposing that Shakespeare could have made use of a Spanish source; and it is not at all probable that a translation was made within a year of the publication in Spain.

Tieck was the first to point out (in his *Deutsches Theater*, 1817) a relation between *The Fair Sidea* and *The Tempest*. The German play was written by Jacob Ayrer, Notarius Publicus and Procurator to the Court in Nuremberg. Ayrer died in 1605, and *The Fair Sidea* was first published in 1618, in a large volume of plays collected and written by him. In this play Duke (or Prince) Ludolff, a magician, has an only daughter, Sidea, and an attendant spirit, Runcifal. He is overcome by his rival, Duke (or Prince) Leudegast, and is driven into a forest. Engelbrecht, son of Leudegast, meets Prince Ludolff and his daughter; refuses to surrender, draws his sword, and is made helpless by the magic power of Ludolff; becomes a servant to Sidea, to carry logs for her. She takes pity on him, and offers to marry him. After various disappearances and returns, the fathers are reconciled.

A brief summary of the German play, as also of the Spanish tale, emphasizes the points of likeness to *The Tempest*, and minimizes the differences, which are numerous and pervasive. In character, atmosphere, spirit, Shakespeare's romance differs greatly from this

dull, prosaic play. It is known that a company of English
actors was at Nuremberg in 1604 and in 1606, and it has
been conjectured that they brought to England this play
or a report of it. More probably *The Tempest, The Fair
Sidea,* and the story of King Dardano, derive from a common source as yet undiscovered.

Various facts of Italian history may have had a bearing
on the story. A real Alonso, King of Naples, was suc-
ceeded in 1495 by his son Ferdinand. A banished Duke
of Milan may be found in Maximilian who was dispossessed in 1514; and an usurping duke in 1477,
— Prospero Adorno, who was established with the aid of
Ferdinand of Naples. These details could have been
found by Shakespeare in the *Historye of Italie* (1549)
by William Thomas. The names Prospero and Stephano
appear in Ben Jonson's *Every Man in His Humour,* in
which Shakespeare was one of the actors. Prospero
was also the name of a riding-master, probably a
Neapolitan, who lived in London in Shakespeare's day.

The speech of Prospero, " Ye elves of hills, brooks,
standing lakes, and groves " (V. i. 33–50), is a para-
phrase of Ovid's *Metamorphoses,* VII, 192–219, a passage
that Shakespeare may have read as a schoolboy at
Stratford. He may have known Ovid better than any other
Latin poet. He certainly made use, however, of the
translation of the *Metamorphoses* by Arthur Golding,
published in 1565; he had already used this translation
in his burlesque dramatization of the story of Pyramus
and Thisbe. There is a striking resemblance between the
speech of Prospero — " And like the baseless fabric,"

etc. (IV. i. 151) and a passage in *The Tragedie of Darius*
(1603), by Sir William Alexander, afterward Earl of
Sterling. Phrases in the speeches of Gonzalo about his
ideal commonwealth (II. i. 147–162) are based upon the
translation by John Florio of Montaigne's *Essays* (I,
30: Of the Caniballes), published in 1603. From other
plays also it is evident that Shakespeare was acquainted
with the *Essays* of Montaigne. Mention has already
been made of the pamphlets by Silvester Jourdan and
William Strachey on the shipwreck of Sir George Somers
and his companions. These and other books of travel
and discovery, such as Eden's *History of Travaile* (1577),
Raleigh's *Discovery of Guiana* (1596), Shakespeare read
and used. There is also the possibility, — probability
one might say, — that in some London tavern he plied
with questions some sailor or colonist who had returned
from the expedition of 1609. What more natural for
a playwright who was working upon a play dealing with
storm and shipwreck? Several months after writing these
words the present editor found a reference to an interesting
letter by Rudyard Kipling in the London *Spectator* of
July 2, 1898. Mr. Kipling suggests that the manager-
playwright may have drawn character, incident, setting,
atmosphere, from "the chatter of a half-tipsy sailor at
a theater," and have fitted them to a play that was already
taking shape in his mind. To the manager-playwright
"in a receptive hour, sent by heaven, entered the original
Stephano, fresh from the seas and half-seas over. To
him Stephano told his tale all in one piece, a two hours'
discourse of most glorious absurdities." The genesis
of atmosphere, minor characters, and underplot, as con-

jectured by the fertile imagination of a writer of our own
day, will repay a careful reading.

Relations to Contemporary Drama. — *The Tempest* is
one of the group of latest plays, — including *Pericles,
Cymbeline,* and *The Winter's Tale,* — that are usually
termed dramatic romances. These plays have in common
the restoration of a lost child, or children, and the recon-
ciliation of parted friends or relatives; in *Pericles* the
loss is caused by a shipwreck. In each of these plays
there is a group of older characters, and a girlish heroine
who is the center of a group of younger characters. Some
critics[1] have discovered in this group of plays the influence
of the early plays of Beaumont and Fletcher, — such as
Philaster. It has also been observed that among the varied
suggestions from which Shakespeare made his play of an
enchanted island, he drew some hints from the very
elaborate Court Masques which were then in high favor
at the Court of James. The betrothal of Ferdinand and
Miranda is celebrated by a masque (IV. i), and the
" strange shapes " (III. iii. divers spirits, IV. i) may have
been suggested by the " antimasques," or grotesque
dances of the Court performances.

Imitations and Adaptations. — *The Tempest* won immediate and continued popularity, as is attested by the
comment of Ben Jonson[2] in the Induction to *Bartholomew*

---

[1] The *Influence of Beaumont and Fletcher on Shakespeare*.
A. H. Thorndike, Worcester, 1901.

[2] If there bee never a *Servant* monster i' the *Fayre* who can
helpe it ? he sayes : nor a nest of *Antiques?* Hee [the author]
is loth to make Nature afraid in his *Playes,* like those that beget
Tales, Tempests, and such like *Drolleries.*

Fair (1614), and by the imitation by Fletcher and Massinger in *The Sea Voyage*. In the preface to the adaptation of *The Tempest* by Dryden and Davenant, Dryden wrote: "Our excellent Fletcher had so great a value for it, that he thought fit to make use of the same Design, not much varied, a second time. Those who have seen his *Sea-Voyage* may easily discern that it was a copy of *Shakespear's Tempest;* the Storm, the Desert Island, and the Woman who had never seen a Man, are all sufficient Testimonies of it. But Fletcher was not the only Poet who made use of *Shakespear's* Plot. Sir John Suckling, a profess'd admirer of our Author, has follow'd his footsteps in his *Goblins;* his *Regmella* being an open imitation of *Shakespear's Miranda;* and his Spirits, though counterfeit, yet are copied from Ariel. But Sir *William Davenant*, as he was a Man of quick and piercing imagination, soon found that somewhat might be added to the design of *Shakespear*, of which neither *Fletcher* nor *Suckling* had ever thought: and therefore to put the last hand to it, he design'd the Counterpart to *Shakespear's* Plot, namely, that of a Man who had never seen a Woman. . . . This excellent Contrivance he was pleased to communicate to me, and to desire my assistance in it." Thus it was that the poet laureate and the laureate to be rewrote *The Tempest* in 1667, to suit the taste of Restoration audiences. Miranda was given a sister, Dorinda, to serve as a confidante; Hippolito, "one that never saw woman," is a counterpart to Miranda. Ariel has a companion spirit, Milcha; Caliban has a sister, Sycorax, who weds Trincalo (*sic*). If Shakespeare could have seen this play, he would indeed have had cause to

say, " Thou art translated." Yet Dryden professed, and
unquestionably felt, the greatest respect and admiration
for Shakespeare.

> The Storm which vanish'd on the neighb'ring shore,
> Was taught by *Shakespear's* Tempest first to roar.
>
> .   .   .   .   .   .
>
> But *Shakespear's* Magick could not copy'd be,
> Within that Circle none durst walk but he.
> I must confess 't was bold, nor would you now
> That liberty to vulgar Wits allow,
> Which work by Magick supernatural things:
> But *Shakespear's* Pow'r is Sacred as a King's.

The *Tempest* of Dryden and Davenant is the play that
Samuel Pepys saw with pleasure some half dozen times.
This Restoration perversion of the play held the stage
for more than one hundred years. It was produced
in the provinces in 1767 by Mr. Kemble's Company of
Comedians: Sarah Kemble (afterwards Mrs. Siddons),
then twelve years old, took the part of Ariel. The same
version was produced by John Kemble at the Drury Lane
Theater in 1789.

The two fairy plays have supplied the largest number
of passages for music. Thirteen passages in *The Tempest*
have been set to music (Furnivall, in the New Shakspere
Society's List, etc., 1884). The music composed in 1612,
by Robert Johnson, for " Full fathom five " (I. ii. 396)
and " Where the bee sucks " (V. i. 88) has been preserved
in Wilson's *Cheerful Ayres or Ballads* (Oxford, 1660).
These settings may have been heard by Shakespeare.
In 1673 *The Tempest* was turned into an opera by Thomas
Shadwell, who made various transpositions and additions,

and an entirely new masque at the close. For this opera, as also for *A Midsummer-Night's Dream*, Henry Purcell, England's greatest composer, wrote music. In February, 1756, this opera was produced by David Garrick; the adaptation was attributed to him then and later, but was disowned by him.

The Tempest is undramatic, and is seldom performed to-day. The opposing forces are too unequal; the spectator feels no anxiety for Prospero, who is all-powerful. If, indeed, his enemies were to gain the upper hand, what complications, what misfortunes might ensue! More significant than the history of occasional performances are the plays and poems that have been suggested by *The Tempest*. Thus F. G. Waldron published in 1797 *The Virgin Queen*, a drama in five acts, "attempted as a sequel to Shakespeare's *Tempest*." In this play Caliban takes advantage of Prospero's mistake in breaking his magic staff and drowning his book; but for the timely help of Ariel, Prospero and Miranda would have been in dire straits. So Ernest Renan wrote, in 1878, *Caliban*, a continuation of *The Tempest*. In this philosophical drama Prospero has returned to his books, and is again neglectful of his duties of state. Caliban, whom Prospero has injudiciously taken with him to Milan, is intended to represent the spirit of social democracy. By instigating a revolution he dethrones Prospero, and usurps his power. Once in power, however, he finds it advisable to carry out — for his own interests — the policies of Prospero. A benevolent despot has been exchanged for a despot who is selfish and brutal.

Interpretation of Characters. — More than in any other
of Shakespeare's dramas the leading characters in this play
are types rather than individuals. Prospero, — the for-
tunate one, — with his serene wisdom is an over-ruling
providence, the divinity of the island. None the less,
trusting unduly in the power of intellect, he has paid
the penalty for giving overmuch time to his books and for
neglecting the cares and duties of everyday life. Though
we sympathize with Prospero as one who has been wronged,
yet we feel no concern for one who can cause the storm
with which the play begins, can call spirits from the
vasty deep, and thus control both man and nature.

Miranda — to be wondered at (I. ii. 426; III. i. 37) —
is pure womanhood. Like Eve in Paradise, a child of
nature, simple, unsophisticated, she has never learned
that she must conceal her feelings. Of about the age of
Juliet, just on the verge of womanhood, unversed in
the arts of court, she knows no reason why she should
hide her love. "I am your wife, if you will marry me;
If not, I'll die your maid" (*i.e.*, maid-servant). Her
girlish innocence is the more apparent because there is no
other woman in the play with whom she may be compared.
Beside Caliban she is an ethereal being; beside Ariel
she is "a Spirit, yet a Woman too." Only the creator
of Lucy Desborough has known how to draw heroines
as adorable as those whom Shakespeare's vision has
brought to life.

The name and description of Ariel — "an ayrie Spirit"
— indicate his native element (cf. V. i. 21). Yet he can
take at will the form of fire (I. ii. 191, 198–200), or at the

command of Prospero the form of a water-nymph (I. ii. 301, 316). Invisible as air, except to Prospero, at times he is only a musical voice. A sexless creature, he is devoid of human feelings. He pleads for liberty; he must be free as air, or as the mountain winds. Yet Prospero's power can control Ariel, can use him as a servant.

Caliban, the servant-monster, "the offspring of an Incubus and a Sorceress" (cf. I. ii. 320), is one of the most remarkable of Shakespeare's creations. Compounded of the downward elements, earth and water (cf. I. ii. 314, 317), he is "of the earth, earthy," brutish, almost animal. At this time of exploration and discovery, when Indians were brought to England and exhibited, much curiosity was felt for the new type of barbarian with which civilization was newly confronted. What was his nature, what his capacity? The answer of our play is to the effect that the noble red man is brutish by nature, that he learns the vices of civilization more readily than its virtues. He is ready to worship Trinculo (*Trinch*) because of the celestial liquor (*vin divin*) that he bestows from his holy bottle; he seeks to violate the honor of Prospero's daughter. Yet though he is unmoral, he is not lacking in understanding. He can be used as a servant; "we cannot miss (*i.e.*, do without) him." He loves sweet music (III. ii. 144–153), and he speaks in verse. It has been suggested that in Caliban (Can-i-bal?) Shakespeare was satirizing the picture of the noble savage that Montaigne had drawn in his essay (I. 30) "Of the Caniballes." In 1873 Dr. Daniel Wilson, of Toronto, published an interesting

study entitled *Caliban: the Missing Link*. "Caliban
seems indeed the half human link between the brute and
the man." "He is not a brutalized, but a natural brute
mind. He is a being in whom the moral instincts of man
have no part; but also in whom the degradation of savage
humanity is equally wanting." Superior in intellect to
the highest animal, he dreads the power of Prospero;
"we shall all be turn'd . . . to apes, with foreheads
villanous low." Browning's *Caliban upon Setebos;
or Natural Theology in the Island* is a keen satire upon
anthropomorphic conceptions of God. Caliban's god,
Setebos, is made in his own image, and is therefore cruel,
malignant, irresponsible.

> As it likes me each time, I do; so He.

Structure and Allegory. — In *The Tempest* the unities
of time and place are closely observed. The action
occupies less than the time 'twixt two o'clock and six.
After the shipwreck the scene is either "before Prospero's
cell" (back scene) or in "another part of the Island"
(front scene). In *The Winter's Tale*, perhaps written
immediately before *The Tempest*, Shakespeare completely disregarded these two unities.

It must be a trustworthy instinct that leads students
of *The Tempest* to see in Prospero the counterpart of
Shakespeare at the close of his career as a dramatist.

> Graves at my command
> Have waked their sleepers, oped, and let 'em forth
> By my so potent art.

The great magician was ready to abjure his art and to break his staff, then to retire to his dukedom, at Stratford, where

> Every third thought shall be my grave.

" *The Tempest*," says Lowell, " is an example of how a great poet should write allegory; " and he remarks that " Poets are always entitled to a royalty on what we find in their works." Lowell [1] has given one interpretation of the allegory; Professor Dowden,[2] another; both see in Prospero Shakespeare bidding farewell to the stage and returning to Stratford. Against adverse circumstances he had struggled bravely, and had achieved greatly. Like Prospero, he was ready to say, —

> We are such stuff
> As dreams are made on, and our little life
> Is rounded with a sleep.

[1] "Shakespeare Once More" in *Among My Books*, Vol. I. Prose Works, III, 60.

[2] *Shakspere; His Mind and Art*, pp. 371–380.

The Tempest

[DRAMATIS PERSONÆ]

ALONSO, king of Naples.
SEBASTIAN, his brother.
PROSPERO, the right duke of Milan.
ANTONIO, his brother, the usurping duke of Milan.
FERDINAND, son to the king of Naples.
GONZALO, an honest old Counsellor.
ADRIAN, } Lords.
FRANCISCO, }
CALIBAN, a savage and deformed Slave.
TRINCULO, a Jester.
STEPHANO, a drunken Butler.
Master of a Ship.
Boatswain.
Mariners.

MIRANDA, daughter to Prospero.

ARIEL, an airy Spirit.

IRIS,
CERES,
JUNO, } Spirits.
Nymphs,
Reapers,

[Other Spirits attending on Prospero.]

SCENE: [A ship at sea;] an uninhabited island.

The Tempest

ACT FIRST

SCENE I

*[On a ship at sea :] a tempestuous noise of thunder and
lightning heard.*

Enter a Ship-Master and a Boatswain.

Mast. Boatswain!

Boats. Here, master; what cheer?

Mast. Good; speak to the mariners. Fall to't,
yarely, or we run ourselves aground. Bestir,
bestir. *Exit.*

Enter Mariners.

Boats. Heigh, my hearts! cheerly, cheerly, my 6
hearts! yare, yare! Take in the topsail. Tend
to the master's whistle. — Blow till thou burst
thy wind, if room enough!

3

Enter Alonso, Sebastian, Antonio, Ferdinand, Gonzalo,
and others.

Alon. Good boatswain, have care. Where's the   10
  master? Play the men.
Boats. I pray now, keep below.
Ant. Where is the master, boatswain?
Boats. Do you not hear him? You mar our labour.
  Keep your cabins; you do assist the storm.   15
Gon. Nay, good, be patient.
Boats. When the sea is. Hence! What cares
  these roarers for the name of king? To cabin!
  silence! trouble us not.
Gon. Good, yet remember whom thou hast   20
  aboard.
Boats. None that I more love than myself. You
  are a counsellor; if you can command these
  elements to silence, and work the peace of the
  present, we will not hand a rope more; use   25
  your authority. If you cannot, give thanks you
  have liv'd so long, and make yourself ready in
  your cabin for the mischance of the hour, if it
  so hap.—Cheerly, good hearts!—Out of our
  way, I say.   *Exit.*
Gon. I have great comfort from this fellow. 30
  Methinks he hath no drowning mark upon
  him; his complexion is perfect gallows.
  Stand fast, good Fate, to his hanging; make

the rope of his destiny our cable, for our
own doth little advantage. If he be not born   35
to be hang'd, our case is miserable.   *Exeunt.*

Re-enter Boatswain.

Boats. Down with the topmast! yare! lower,
     lower! Bring her to try wi' the main-course.
     A plague   (*A cry within.*)

Enter Sebastian, Antonio, and Gonzalo.

upon this howling! They are louder than the
     weather or our office. — Yet again! What   40
     do you here? Shall we give o'er and drown?
     Have you a mind to sink?
Seb. A pox o' your throat, you bawling, blas-
     phemous, incharitable dog!
Boats. Work you, then.   45
Ant. Hang, cur! hang, you whoreson, insolent
     noisemaker! We are less afraid to be drown'd
     than thou art.
Gon. I'll warrant him for drowning though the
     ship were no stronger than a nut-shell and   50
     as leaky as an unstanched wench.
Boats. Lay her a-hold, a-hold! Set her two
     courses off to sea again! Lay her off.

Enter Mariners wet.

Mariners. All lost! To prayers, to prayers!
     All lost!   55
Boats. What, must our mouths be cold?
Gon. The King and Prince at prayers! Let's
     assist them,
     For our case is as theirs.
Seb.   I'm out of patience.
Ant. We are merely cheated of our lives by drunkards.
     This wide-chapp'd rascal — would thou mightst
     lie drowning   60
     The washing of ten tides!
Gon.   He'll be hang'd yet,
     Though every drop of water swear against it
     And gape at wid'st to glut him.
                A confused noise within.
     Mercy on us!
     We split, we split! Farewell, my wife and
     children!   65
     Farewell, brother! We split, we split, we split!
Ant. Let's all sink wi' the King.
Seb. Let's take leave of him.   *Exit.*
Gon. Now would I give a thousand furlongs of
     sea for an acre of barren ground, long heath,   70
     brown furze, anything. The wills above be
     done! but I would fain die a dry death.
                       Exeunt.

SCENE II

[The island. Before Prospero's cell.]

Enter Prospero and Miranda.

Mir. If by your art, my dearest father, you have
    Put the wild waters in this roar, allay them.
    The sky, it seems, would pour down stinking
      pitch,
    But that the sea, mounting to the welkin's
      cheek,
    Dashes the fire out. O, I have suffered   5
    With those that I saw suffer! A brave vessel,
    Who had, no doubt, some noble creature in her,
    Dash'd all to pieces! O, the cry did knock
    Against my very heart. Poor souls, they per-
      ish'd.
    Had I been any god of power, I would   10
    Have sunk the sea within the earth or ere
    It should the good ship so have swallow'd and
    The fraughting souls within her.

Pros.   Be collected;
    No more amazement. Tell your piteous heart
    There's no harm done.

Mir.   O, woe the day!

Pros.   No harm.
    I have done nothing but in care of thee,   16
    Of thee, my dear one, thee, my daughter, who

Art ignorant of what thou art, nought know-
    ing
Of whence I am, nor that I am more better
Than Prospero, master of a full poor cell,   20
And thy no greater father.

Mir.   More to know
Did never meddle with my thoughts.

Pros.   'Tis time
I should inform thee farther. Lend thy hand,
And pluck my magic garment from me. So,
                         [*Lays down his mantle.*]
Lie there, my art. Wipe thou thine eyes; have
    comfort.   25
The direful spectacle of the wreck, which touch'd
The very virtue of compassion in thee,
I have with such provision in mine art
So safely ordered that there is no soul —
No, not so much perdition as an hair   30
Betid to any creature in the vessel
Which thou heard'st cry, which thou saw'st sink.
    Sit down;
For thou must now know farther.

Mir.   You have often
Begun to tell me what I am, but stopp'd
And left me to a bootless inquisition,   35
Concluding, "Stay, not yet."

Pros.   The hour's now come;
The very minute bids thee ope thine ear.

Obey and be attentive.   Canst thou remember
A time before we came unto this cell?
I do not think thou canst, for then thou wast not 40
Out three years old.

Mir.   Certainly, sir, I can.

Pros. By what?   By any other house or person?
Of anything the image tell me, that
Hath kept with thy remembrance.

Mir.   'Tis far off
And rather like a dream than an assurance   45
That my remembrance warrants.   Had I not
Four or five women once that tended me?

Pros. Thou hadst, and more, Miranda.   But how is
     it
That this lives in thy mind?   What seest thou
     else
In the dark backward and abysm of time?   50
If thou rememb'rest aught ere thou cam'st here,
How thou cam'st here thou may'st.

Mir.   But that I do not.

Pros. Twelve year since, Miranda, twelve year since,
Thy father was the Duke of Milan and   54
A prince of power.

Mir.   Sir, are not you my father?

Pros. Thy mother was a piece of virtue, and
She said thou wast my daughter; and thy father
Was Duke of Milan, and his only heir
And princess no worse issued.

Mir. O the heavens!
What foul play had we, that we came from
thence? 60
Or blessed was't we did?

Pros. Both, both, my girl.
By foul play, as thou say'st, were we heav'd
thence,
But blessedly holp hither.

Mir. O, my heart bleeds
To think o' the teen that I have turn'd you to,
Which is from my remembrance! Please you,
farther. 65

Pros. My brother and thy uncle, call'd Antonio —
I pray thee, mark me — that a brother should
Be so perfidious! — he whom next thyself
Of all the world I lov'd, and to him put
The manage of my state; as at that time 70
Through all the signories it was the first,
And Prospero the prime duke, being so reputed
In dignity, and for the liberal arts
Without a parallel; those being all my study,
The government I cast upon my brother 75
And to my state grew stranger, being trans-
ported
And rapt in secret studies. Thy false uncle —
Dost thou attend me?

Mir. Sir, most heedfully.

Pros. Being once perfected how to grant suits,

How to deny them, who to advance and who   80
To trash for overtopping, new created
The creatures that were mine, I say, or chang'd
     'em,
Or else new form'd 'em; having both the key
Of officer and office, set all hearts i' the state
To what tune pleas'd his ear; that now he was   85
The ivy which had hid my princely trunk,
And suck'd my verdure out on't. Thou at-
     tend'st not.

Mir.   O, good sir, I do.

Pros.   I pray thee, mark me.
I, thus neglecting worldly ends, all dedicated
To closeness and the bettering of my mind   90
With that which, but by being so retir'd,
O'er-priz'd all popular rate, in my false brother
Awak'd an evil nature; and my trust,
Like a good parent, did beget of him
A falsehood, in its contrary as great   95
As my trust was; which had indeed no limit,
A confidence sans bound. He being thus lorded,
Not only with what my revenue yielded,
But what my power might else exact, — like one
Who having into truth, by telling of it,   100
Made such a sinner of his memory
To credit his own lie, — he did believe
He was indeed the Duke. Out o' the substitu-
     tion,

And executing the outward face of royalty,
With all prerogative, hence his ambition grow-
    ing —   105
Dost thou hear?

Mir.   Your tale, sir, would cure deafness.

Pros. To have no screen between this part he
    play'd
And him he play'd it for, he needs will be
Absolute Milan. Me, poor man! — my library
Was dukedom large enough — of temporal royal-
    ties   110
He thinks me now incapable; confederates —
So dry he was for sway — wi' the King of
    Naples
To give him annual tribute, do him homage,
Subject his coronet to his crown, and bend
The dukedom yet unbow'd — alas, poor Mi-
    lan! —   115
To most ignoble stooping.

Mir.   O the heavens!

Pros. Mark his condition and the event, then tell
    me
If this might be a brother.

Mir.   I should sin
To think but nobly of my grandmother.
Good wombs have borne bad sons.

Pros.   Now the condition.
This King of Naples, being an enemy   121

To me inveterate, hearkens my brother's suit;
Which was, that he, in lieu o' the premises,
Of homage and I know not how much tribute,
Should presently extirpate me and mine   125
Out of the dukedom, and confer fair Milan
With all the honours on my brother; whereon,
A treacherous army levied, one midnight
Fated to the purpose did Antonio open
The gates of Milan; and, i' the dead of darkness,   130
The ministers for the purpose hurried thence
Me and thy crying self.

Mir.   Alack, for pity!
I, not rememb'ring how I cried out then,
Will cry it o'er again. It is a hint   134
That wrings mine eyes to't.

Pros.   Hear a little further,
And then I'll bring thee to the present business
Which now's upon's, without the which this story
Were most impertinent.

Mir.   Wherefore did they not
That hour destroy us?

Pros.   Well demanded, wench;
My tale provokes that question. Dear, they durst not   140
(So dear the love my people bore me) set
A mark so bloody on the business; but

With colours fairer painted their foul ends.

In few, they hurried us aboard a bark,

Bore us some leagues to sea; where they pre-
    pared   145

A rotten carcass of a butt, not rigg'd,

Nor tackle, sail, nor mast; the very rats

Instinctively have quit it. There they hoist us,

To cry to the sea that roar'd to us, to sigh

To the winds whose pity, sighing back again, 150

Did us but loving wrong.

Mir.   Alack, what trouble

Was I then to you !

Pros.   O, a cherubin

Thou wast that did preserve me. Thou didst
    smile,

Infused with a fortitude from heaven,

When I have deck'd the sea with drops full
    salt,   155

Under my burden groan'd; which rais'd in me

An undergoing stomach, to bear up

Against what should ensue.

Mir.   How came we ashore?

Pros. By Providence divine.

Some food we had and some fresh water
    that   160

A noble Neapolitan, Gonzalo,

Out of his charity, who being then appointed

Master of this design, did give us, with

Rich garments, linens, stuffs, and necessaries,
Which since have steaded much; so, of his gentle-
  ness,   165
Knowing I lov'd my books, he furnish'd me
From mine own library with volumes that
I prize above my dukedom.

Mir.   Would I might

  But ever see that man!

Pros.   Now I arise.

            [*Puts on his robe.*]

Sit still, and hear the last of our sea-sorrow. 170
Here in this island we arriv'd; and here
Have I, thy schoolmaster, made thee more profit
Than other princess can that have more time
For vainer hours, and tutors not so careful.

Mir. Heavens thank you for't! And now, I pray
  you, sir,   175
For still 'tis beating in my mind, your reason
For raising this sea-storm?

Pros.   Know thus far forth.

By accident most strange, bountiful Fortune,
Now my dear lady, hath mine enemies
Brought to this shore; and by my prescience 180
I find my zenith doth depend upon
A most auspicious star, whose influence
If now I court not but omit, my fortunes
Will ever after droop. Here cease more ques-
  tions.

Thou art inclin'd to sleep; 'tis a good dulness, 185
And give it way. I know thou canst not choose.
[*Miranda sleeps.*]
Come away, servant, come; I am ready now.
Approach, my Ariel; come.

Enter Ariel.

Ari. All hail, great master! grave sir, hail! I come
To answer thy best pleasure, be't to fly, 190
To swim, to dive into the fire, to ride
On the curl'd clouds. To thy strong bidding
task
Ariel and all his quality.
Pros. Hast thou, spirit,
Perform'd to point the tempest that I bade
thee?
Ari. To every article. 195
I boarded the king's ship; now on the beak,
Now in the waist, the deck, in every cabin,
I flam'd amazement. Sometime I'd divide,
And burn in many places. On the topmast,
The yards and bowsprit, would I flame dis-
tinctly, 200
Then meet and join. Jove's lightnings, the pre-
cursors
O' the dreadful thunder-claps, more momentary
And sight-outrunning were not; the fire and
cracks

Of sulphurous roaring the most mighty Neptune
Seem to besiege, and make his bold waves
    tremble,   205
Yea, his dread trident shake.

Pros.   My brave spirit !
Who was so firm, so constant, that this coil
Would not infect his reason ?

Ari.   Not a soul
But felt a fever of the mad, and play'd
Some tricks of desperation. All but mariners 210
Plung'd in the foaming brine and quit the vessel,
Then all afire with me. The King's son, Ferdi-
    nand,
With hair up-staring, — then like reeds, not
    hair, —
Was the first man that leap'd; cried, "Hell is
    empty,   214
And all the devils are here."

Pros.   Why, that's my spirit !
But was not this nigh shore ?

Ari.   Close by, my master.

Pros. But are they, Ariel, safe ?

Ari.   Not a hair perish'd ;
On their sustaining garments not a blemish,
But fresher than before ; and, as thou bad'st me,
In troops I have dispers'd them 'bout the
    isle.   220
The King's son have I landed by himself,

    C

Whom I left cooling of the air with sighs
In an odd angle of the isle, and sitting,
His arms in this sad knot.

Pros.   Of the King's ship
The mariners say how thou hast dispos'd,   225
And all the rest o' the fleet.

Ari.   Safely in harbour
Is the King's ship; in the deep nook, where
    once
Thou call'dst me up at midnight to fetch dew
From the still-vex'd Bermoothes, there she's hid;
The mariners all under hatches stow'd,   230
Who, with a charm join'd to their suff'red la-
    bour,
I have left asleep; and for the rest o' the fleet,
Which I dispers'd, they all have met again,
And are upon the Mediterranean float
Bound sadly home for Naples,   235
Supposing that they saw the King's ship
    wreck'd
And his great person perish.

Pros.   Ariel, thy charge
Exactly is perform'd; but there's more work.
What is the time o' the day?

Ari.   Past the mid season.

Pros. At least two glasses. The time 'twixt six and
    now   240
Must by us both be spent most preciously.

Ari. Is there more toil? Since thou dost give me
      pains,
    Let me remember thee what thou hast promis'd,
    Which is not yet perform'd me.

Pros.   How now? moody?
    What is't thou canst demand?

Ari.   My liberty. 245

Pros. Before the time be out? No more!

Ari.   I prithee,
    Remember I have done thee worthy service,
    Told thee no lies, made thee no mistakings, serv'd
    Without or grudge or grumblings. Thou did
      promise
    To bate me a full year.

Pros.   Dost thou forget 250
    From what a torment I did free thee?

Ari.   No.

Pros. Thou dost, and think'st it much to tread the
      ooze
    Of the salt deep,
    To run upon the sharp wind of the north,
    To do me business in the veins o' the earth 255
    When it is bak'd with frost.

Ari.   I do not, sir.

Pros. Thou liest, malignant thing! Hast thou forgot
    The foul witch Sycorax, who with age and envy
    Was grown into a hoop? Hast thou forgot her?

Ari. No, sir.

Pros. Thou hast. Where was she born? Speak;
    tell me. 260

Ari. Sir, in Argier.

Pros.   O, was she so? I must
    Once in a month recount what thou hast been,
    Which thou forget'st. This damn'd witch Sycorax,
    For mischiefs manifold and sorceries terrible
    To enter human hearing, from Argier, 265
    Thou know'st, was banish'd; for one thing she did
    They would not take her life. Is not this true?

Ari. Ay, sir.

Pros. This blue-ey'd hag was hither brought with child,
    And here was left by the sailors. Thou, my slave,
    As thou report'st thyself, was then her servant; 271
    And, for thou wast a spirit too delicate
    To act her earthy and abhorr'd commands,
    Refusing her grand hests, she did confine thee,
    By help of her more potent ministers 275
    And in her most unmitigable rage,
    Into a cloven pine; within which rift
    Imprison'd thou didst painfully remain
    A dozen years; within which space she died
    And left thee there, where thou didst vent thy groans
    As fast as mill-wheels strike. Then was this
       island — 281
    Save for the son that she did litter here,
    A freckl'd whelp, hag-born, — not honour'd with
    A human shape.

Ari.   Yes, Caliban her son.

Pros. Dull thing, I say so; he, that Caliban   285
    Whom now I keep in service. Thou best know'st
    What torment I did find thee in; thy groans
    Did make wolves howl, and penetrate the breasts
    Of ever angry bears. It was a torment
    To lay upon the damn'd, which Sycorax   290
    Could not again undo. It was mine art,
    When I arriv'd and heard thee, that made gape
    The pine, and let thee out.

Ari.   I thank thee, master.

Pros. If thou more murmur'st, I will rend an oak
    And peg thee in his knotty entrails till   295
    Thou hast howl'd away twelve winters.

Ari.   Pardon, master;
    I will be correspondent to command
    And do my spiriting gently.

Pros.   Do so, and after two days
    I will discharge thee.

Ari.   That's my noble master!
    What shall I do? say what. What shall I do? 300

Pros. Go make thyself like a nymph o' the sea; be subject
    To no sight but thine and mine, invisible
    To every eyeball else. Go take this shape
    And hither come in't. Go, hence with diligence!

                           Exit Ariel.

    Awake, dear heart, awake! Thou hast slept well;
    Awake!

Mir.   The strangeness of your story put 306
    Heaviness in me.

Pros.   Shake it off.   Come on,
    We'll visit Caliban my slave, who never
    Yields us kind answer.

Mir.   'Tis a villain, sir,
    I do not love to look on.

Pros.   But, as 'tis, 310
    We cannot miss him.   He does make our fire,
    Fetch in our wood, and serves in offices
    That profit us.   What, ho! slave!   Caliban!
    Thou earth, thou! speak.

Cal.   (*Within.*) There's wood enough within.

Pros. Come forth, I say! there's other business for
       thee. 315
    Come, thou tortoise! when?

Re-enter Ariel like a water-nymph.

    Fine apparition!   My quaint Ariel,
    Hark in thine ear.

Ari.   My lord, it shall be done.

                                       Exit.

Pros. Thou poisonous slave, got by the devil himself
    Upon thy wicked dam, come forth! 320

Enter Caliban.

Cal. As wicked dew as e'er my mother brush'd
    With raven's feather from unwholesome fen

Drop on you both !   A south-west blow on ye
And blister you all o'er !

Pros. For this, be sure, to-night thou shalt have
       cramps,   325
Side-stitches that shall pen thy breath up ; urchins
Shall, for that vast of night that they may work,
All exercise on thee ; thou shalt be pinch'd
As thick as honeycomb, each pinch more stinging
Than bees that made 'em.

Cal.   I must eat my dinner.
This island's mine, by Sycorax my mother,   331
Which thou tak'st from me.   When thou cam'st
       first,
Thou strok'dst me and made much of me, wouldst
       give me
Water with berries in't, and teach me how
To name the bigger light, and how the less,   335
That burn by day and night ; and then I lov'd thee
And show'd thee all the qualities o' the isle,
The fresh springs, brine-pits, barren place and fer-
       tile.
Curs'd be I that did so !   All the charms
Of Sycorax, toads, beetles, bats, light on you ! 340
For I am all the subjects that you have,
Which first was mine own king ; and here you sty
       me
In this hard rock, whiles you do keep from me
The rest o' the island.

Pros.   Thou most lying slave,

     Whom stripes may move, not kindness! I have
         us'd thee,   345

     Filth as thou art, with human care, and lodg'd thee

     In mine own cell, till thou didst seek to violate

     The honour of my child.

Cal. O ho, O ho! would't had been done!

     Thou didst prevent me; I had peopl'd else   350

     This isle with Calibans.

[*Pros.*]   Abhorred slave,

     Which any print of goodness wilt not take,

     Being capable of all ill! I pitied thee,

     Took pains to make thee speak, taught thee each
         hour   354

     One thing or other. When thou didst not, savage,

     Know thine own meaning, but wouldst gabble like

     A thing most brutish, I endow'd thy purposes

     With words that made them known. But thy vile
         race,

     Though thou didst learn, had that in't which good
         natures

     Could not abide to be with; therefore wast thou 360

     Deservedly confin'd into this rock,

     Who hadst deserv'd more than a prison.

Cal. You taught me language; and my profit on't

     Is, I know how to curse. The red plague rid you 364

     For learning me your language!

Pros.   Hag-seed, hence!

Fetch us in fuel; and be quick, thou'rt best,
To answer other business.   Shrug'st thou, malice?
If thou neglect'st or dost unwillingly
What I command, I'll rack thee with old cramps,
Fill all thy bones with aches, make thee roar   370
That beasts shall tremble at thy din.

Cal.   No, pray thee.
[*Aside.*] I must obey.   His art is of such power
It would control my dam's god, Setebos,
And make a vassal of him.

Pros.   So, slave; hence! 374
                          Exit Caliban.

Re-enter Ariel, invisible, playing and singing; Ferdinand
[following].

ARIEL'S SONG.

Come unto these yellow sands,
     And then take hands.
Curtsied when you have and kiss'd,
     The wild waves whist,
Foot it featly here and there,   380
And, sweet sprites, the burden bear.

Burden (*dispersedly*).   Hark, hark!
                     Bow-wow.
   The watch-dogs bark!
                     Bow-wow.

Ari. Hark, hark! I hear
    The strain of strutting chanticleer   385
    Cry, "Cock-a-diddle-dow."
Fer. Where should this music be? I' the air or the
        earth?
    It sounds no more; and, sure, it waits upon
    Some god o' the island. Sitting on a bank,
    Weeping again the King my father's wreck,   390
    This music crept by me upon the waters,
    Allaying both their fury and my passion
    With its sweet air; thence I have follow'd it,
    Or it hath drawn me rather. But 'tis gone.
    No, it begins again.   395

ARIEL'S SONG.

    Full fathom five thy father lies;
        Of his bones are coral made;
    Those are pearls that were his eyes:
        Nothing of him that doth fade
    But doth suffer a sea-change   400
    Into something rich and strange.
    Sea-nymphs hourly ring his knell:

Burden. Ding-dong.
[*Ari.*] Hark! now I hear them, — ding-dong, bell.
Fer. The ditty does remember my drown'd father. 405
    This is no mortal business, nor no sound
    That the earth owes. I hear it now above me.

Pros. The fringed curtains of thine eye advance
    And say what thou seest yond.

Mir.   What is't?   A spirit?
    Lord, how it looks about!   Believe me, sir,   410
    It carries a brave form.   But 'tis a spirit.

Pros. No, wench; it eats and sleeps and hath such senses
    As we have, such.   This gallant which thou seest
    Was in the wreck; and, but he's something stain'd
    With grief, that's beauty's canker, thou mightst
        call him   415
    A goodly person.   He hath lost his fellows
    And strays about to find 'em.

Mir.   I might call him
    A thing divine; for nothing natural
    I ever saw so noble.

Pros.   [*Aside.*] It goes on, I see,
    As my soul prompts it. Spirit, fine spirit!   I'll
        free thee   420
    Within two days for this.

Fer.   Most sure, the goddess
    On whom these airs attend!   Vouchsafe my prayer
    May know if you remain upon this island,
    And that you will some good instruction give
    How I may bear me here.   My prime request, 425
    Which I do last pronounce, is, O you wonder!
    If you be maid or no?

Mir.   No wonder, sir,
    But certainly a maid.

Fer.   My language ! heavens !
I am the best of them that speak this speech,
Were I but where 'tis spoken.

Pros.   How ? the best ?
What wert thou, if the King of Naples heard thee ?

Fer. A single thing, as I am now, that wonders   432
To hear thee speak of Naples.   He does hear me ;
And that he does I weep.   Myself am Naples,
Who with mine eyes, never since at ebb, beheld 435
The King my father wreck'd.

Mir.   Alack, for mercy !

Fer. Yes, faith, and all his lords ; the Duke of Milan
And his brave son being twain.

Pros.   [*Aside.*] The Duke of Milan
And his more braver daughter could control thee,
If now 'twere fit to do't.   At the first sight   440
They have chang'd eyes.   Delicate Ariel,
I'll set thee free for this.   [*To Fer.*]   A word, good
    sir ;
I fear you have done yourself some wrong ; a word.

Mir. Why speaks my father so ungently ?   This
Is the third man that e'er I saw, the first   445
That e'er I sigh'd for.   Pity move my father
To be inclin'd my way !

Fer.   O, if a virgin,
And your affection not gone forth, I'll make you
The Queen of Naples.

Pros.   Soft, sir ! one word more.

[*Aside.*] They are both in either's powers; but
    this swift business   450
I must uneasy make, lest too light winning
Make the prize light.   [*To Fer.*] One word more;
    I charge thee
That thou attend me.   Thou dost here usurp
The name thou ow'st not; and hast put thyself
Upon this island as a spy, to win it   455
From me, the lord on't.

Fer.   No, as I am a man.

Mir. There's nothing ill can dwell in such a temple.
If the ill spirit have so fair a house,
Good things will strive to dwell with't.

Pros.   Follow me.
Speak not you for him; he's a traitor.   Come, 460
I'll manacle thy neck and feet together.
Sea-water shalt thou drink; thy food shall be
The fresh-brook mussels, wither'd roots and husks
Wherein the acorn cradled.   Follow.

Fer.   No;
I will resist such entertainment till   465
Mine enemy has more power.

        He draws, and is charmed from moving.

Mir.   O dear father,
Make not too rash a trial of him, for
He's gentle and not fearful.

Pros.   What! I say;
My foot my tutor?   Put thy sword up, traitor,

Who mak'st a show but dar'st not strike, thy con-
 science   470
Is so possess'd with guilt. Come from thy ward,
For I can here disarm thee with this stick
And make thy weapon drop.

Mir.   Beseech you, father.

Pros. Hence ! hang not on my garments.

Mir.   Sir, have pity ;
I'll be his surety.

Pros.   Silence ! one word more   475
Shall make me chide thee, if not hate thee. What !
An advocate for an impostor ! hush !
Thou think'st there is no more such shapes as he,
Having seen but him and Caliban. Foolish
 wench !
To the most of men this is a Caliban,   480
And they to him are angels.

Mir.   My affections
Are then most humble ; I have no ambition
To see a goodlier man.

Pros.   Come on ; obey.
Thy nerves are in their infancy again
And have no vigour in them.

Fer.   So they are.   485
My spirits, as in a dream, are all bound up.
My father's loss, the weakness which I feel,
The wreck of all my friends, nor this man's threats,
To whom I am subdu'd, are but light to me,

Might I but through my prison once a day   490
Behold this maid.   All corners else o' the earth
Let liberty make use of ; space enough
Have I in such a prison.

Pros.   [*Aside.*] It works. [*To Fer.*] Come on.
   —Thou hast done well, fine Ariel ! [*To Fer.*]
     Follow me.
   [*To Ari.*] Hark what thou else shalt do me.

Mir.   Be of comfort ;
My father's of a better nature, sir,   496
Than he appears by speech.   This is unwonted
Which now came from him.

Pros.   [*To Ari.*] Thou shalt be as free
As mountain winds ; but then exactly do
All points of my command.

Ari.   To the syllable.   500

Pros. [*To Mir. and Fer.*] Come, follow. Speak not for
     him.   *Exeunt.*

ACT SECOND

SCENE I

[Another part of the island.]

*Enter Alonso, Sebastian, Antonio, Gonzalo, Adrian,
Francisco, and others.*

Gon. Beseech you, sir, be merry ; you have cause,
   So have we all, of joy ; for our escape
   Is much beyond our loss. Our hint of woe
   Is common ; every day some sailor's wife,
   The masters of some merchant, and the merchant 5
   Have just our theme of woe ; but for the miracle,
   I mean our preservation, few in millions
   Can speak like us. Then wisely, good sir, weigh
   Our sorrow with our comfort.

Alon.   Prithee, peace.

Seb. He receives comfort like cold porridge.   10

Ant. The visitor will not give him o'er so.

Seb. Look, he's winding up the watch of his wit ;
   by and by it will strike.

Gon. Sir, —

Seb. One. Tell.   15

Gon. When every grief is entertain'd that's offer'd,
   Comes to the entertainer —

Seb. A dollar.

Gon. Dolour comes to him, indeed; you have
    spoken truer than you purpos'd.   20

Seb. You have taken it wiselier than I meant you
    should.

Gon. Therefore, my lord, —

Ant. Fie, what a spendthrift is he of his tongue!

Alon. I prithee, spare.   25

Gon. Well, I have done. But yet, —

Seb. He will be talking.

Ant. Which, of he or Adrian, for a good wager,
    first begins to crow?

Seb. The old cock.   30

Ant. The cockerel.

Seb. Done. The wager?

Ant. A laughter.

Seb. A match!

Adr. Though this island seem to be desert, —   35

Seb. Ha, ha, ha! Antonio! So you're paid.

Adr. Uninhabitable and almost inaccessible, —

Seb. Yet, —

Adr. Yet, —

Ant. He could not miss't.   40

Adr. It must needs be of subtle, tender, and deli-
    cate temperance.

Ant. Temperance was a delicate wench.

Seb. Ay, and a subtle; as he most learnedly de-
    liver'd.   45

    D

Adr. The air breathes upon us here most sweetly.

Seb. As if it had lungs and rotten ones.

Ant. Or as 'twere perfum'd by a fen.

Gon. Here is everything advantageous to life.

Ant. True ; save means to live.   50

Seb. Of that there's none, or little.

Gon. How lush and lusty the grass looks ! How green !

Ant. The ground indeed is tawny.

Seb. With an eye of green in't.   55

Ant. He misses not much.

Seb. No ; he doth but mistake the truth totally.

Gon. But the rarity of it is, — which is indeed almost beyond credit, —

Seb. As many vouch'd rarities are.   60

Gon. That our garments, being, as they were, drench'd in the sea, hold notwithstanding their freshness and glosses, being rather new-dy'd than stain'd with salt water.

Ant. If but one of his pockets could speak, would   65 it not say he lies ?

Seb. Ay, or very falsely pocket up his report.

Gon. Methinks our garments are now as fresh as when we put them on first in Afric, at the marriage of the King's fair daughter Claribel   70 to the King of Tunis.

Seb. 'Twas a sweet marriage, and we prosper well in our return.

Adr. Tunis was never grac'd before with such a
    paragon to their queen.   75

Gon. Not since widow Dido's time.

Ant. Widow! a pox o' that! How came that
    widow in? Widow Dido!

Seb. What if he had said "widower Æneas" too?
    Good Lord, how you take it!   80

Adr. "Widow Dido" said you? You make me
    study of that. She was of Carthage, not of
    Tunis.

Gon. This Tunis, sir, was Carthage.

Adr. Carthage?

Gon. I assure you, Carthage.   85

Ant. His word is more than the miraculous harp.

Seb. He hath rais'd the wall and houses too.

Ant. What impossible matter will he make easy
    next?

Seb. I think he will carry this island home in his   90
    pocket and give it his son for an apple.

Ant. And, sowing the kernels of it in the sea, bring
    forth more islands.

Gon. Ay.

Ant. Why, in good time.   95

Gon. Sir, we were talking that our garments seem
    now as fresh as when we were at Tunis at the
    marriage of your daughter, who is now Queen.

Ant. And the rarest that e'er came there.

Seb. Bate, I beseech you, widow Dido.   100

Ant. O, widow Dido! ay, widow Dido.

Gon. Is not, sir, my doublet as fresh as the first day
     I wore it? I mean, in a sort.

Ant. That sort was well fish'd for.

Gon. When I wore it at your daughter's marriage? 105

Alon. You cram these words into mine ears against
     The stomach of my sense. Would I had never
     Married my daughter there! for, coming thence,
     My son is lost and, in my rate, she too,
     Who is so far from Italy removed   110
     I ne'er again shall see her. O thou mine heir
     Of Naples and of Milan, what strange fish
     Hath made his meal on thee?

Fran.   Sir, he may live.
     I saw him beat the surges under him,
     And ride upon their backs. He trod the water,
     Whose enmity he flung aside, and breasted   116
     The surge most swoln that met him. His bold head
     'Bove the contentious waves he kept, and oared
     Himself with his good arms in lusty stroke
     To the shore, that o'er his wave-worn basis bowed,
     As stooping to relieve him. I not doubt   121
     He came alive to land.

Alon.   No, no, he's gone.

Seb. Sir, you may thank yourself for this great loss,
     That would not bless our Europe with your
         daughter,
     But rather lose her to an African;   125

Where she at least is banish'd from your eye,
Who hath cause to wet the grief on't.

Alon.   Prithee, peace.

Seb. You were kneel'd to and importun'd otherwise
By all of us, and the fair soul herself
Weigh'd between loathness and obedience, at   130
Which end o' the beam should bow.   We have lost
    your son,
I fear, for ever.   Milan and Naples have
Moe widows in them of this business' making
Than we bring men to comfort them.
The fault's your own.

Alon.   So is the dear'st o' the loss.

Gon. My lord Sebastian,   136
The truth you speak doth lack some gentleness
And time to speak it in.   You rub the sore,
When you should bring the plaster.

Seb.   Very well.

Ant. And most chirurgeonly.   140

Gon. It is foul weather in us all, good sir,
When you are cloudy.

Seb.   Foul weather ?

Ant.   Very foul.

Gon. Had I plantation of this isle, my lord, —

Ant. He'd sow't with nettle-seed.

Seb.   Or docks, or mallows.

Gon. And were the king on't, what would I do ?   145

Seb. Scape being drunk for want of wine.

Gon. I' the commonwealth I would by contraries
    Execute all things ; for no kind of traffic
    Would I admit ; no name of magistrate ;
    Letters should not be known ; riches, poverty, 150
    And use of service, none ; contract, succession,
    Bourn, bound of land, tilth, vineyard, none ;
    No use of metal, corn, or wine, or oil ;
    No occupation ; all men idle, all ;
    And women too, but innocent and pure ;   155
    No sovereignty ; —

Seb.   Yet he would be king on't.

Ant. The latter end of his commonwealth forgets
    the beginning.

Gon. All things in common nature should produce
    Without sweat or endeavour : treason, felony, 160
    Sword, pike, knife, gun, or need of any engine,
    Would I not have ; but nature should bring forth,
    Of it own kind, all foison, all abundance,
    To feed my innocent people.

Seb. No marrying 'mong his subjects ?   165

Ant. None, man ; all idle ; whores and knaves.

Gon. I would with such perfection govern, sir,
    To excel the golden age.

Seb.   Save his Majesty !

Ant. Long live Gonzalo !

Gon.   And, — do you mark me, sir ?

Alon. Prithee, no more ; thou dost talk nothing to 170
    me.

Gon. I do well believe your Highness ; and did it
     to minister occasion to these gentlemen, who
     are of such sensible and nimble lungs that they
     always use to laugh at nothing.   175

Ant. 'Twas you we laugh'd at.

Gon. Who in this kind of merry fooling am nothing
     to you.   So you may continue and laugh at
     nothing still.

Ant. What a blow was there given !   180

Seb. And it had not fallen flatlong.

Gon. You are gentlemen of brave mettle ; you would
     lift the moon out of her sphere, if she would
     continue in it five weeks without changing.

    Enter Ariel [invisible], playing solemn music.

Seb. We would so, and then go a bat-fowling.   185

Ant. Nay, good my lord, be not angry.

Gon. No, I warrant you ; I will not adventure my
     discretion   so   weakly.   Will   you   laugh   me
     asleep, for I am very heavy ?

Ant. Go sleep, and hear us.   190
         [All sleep except Alon., Seb., and Ant.]

Alon. What, all so soon asleep !   I wish mine eyes
     Would, with themselves, shut up my thoughts.
       I find
     They are inclin'd to do so.

Seb.   Please you, sir,
     Do not omit the heavy offer of it.

It seldom visits sorrow ; when it doth,   195
It is a comforter.

Ant.   We two, my lord,
Will guard your person while you take your rest,
And watch your safety.

Alon.   Thank you.   Wondrous heavy.

                    [*Alonso sleeps.   Exit Ariel.*]

Seb. What a strange drowsiness possesses them !

Ant. It is the quality o' the climate.

Seb.   Why   200
Doth it not then our eyelids sink ? I find not
Myself dispos'd to sleep.

Ant.   Nor I ; my spirits are nimble.
They fell together all, as by consent ;
They dropp'd, as by a thunder-stroke. What might,
Worthy Sebastian, O, what might — ? No
    more : —   205
And yet methinks I see it in thy face,
What thou shouldst be.   The occasion speaks thee,
    and
My strong imagination sees a crown
Dropping upon thy head.

Seb.   What, art thou waking ?

Ant. Do you not hear me speak ?

Seb.   I do ; and surely
It is a sleepy language, and thou speak'st   211
Out of thy sleep.   What is it thou didst say ?
This is a strange repose, to be asleep

With eyes wide open ; standing, speaking, moving,
And yet so fast asleep.

Ant.   Noble Sebastian,   215
Thou let'st thy fortune sleep — die, rather ; wink'st
Whiles thou art waking.

Seb.   Thou dost snore distinctly ;
There's meaning in thy snores.

Ant. I am more serious than my custom ; you
Must be so too, if heed me ; which to do   220
Trebles thee o'er.

Seb.   Well, I am standing water.

Ant. I'll teach you how to flow.

Seb.   Do so. To ebb
Hereditary sloth instructs me.

Ant.   O,
If you but knew how you the purpose cherish
Whiles thus you mock it ! how, in stripping it, 225
You more invest it ! Ebbing men, indeed,
Most often do so near the bottom run
By their own fear or sloth.

Seb.   Prithee, say on.
The setting of thine eye and cheek proclaim
A matter from thee, and a birth indeed   230
Which throes thee much to yield.

Ant.   Thus, sir :
Although this lord of weak remembrance, this,
Who shall be of as little memory
When he is earth'd, hath here almost persuaded —

For he's a spirit of persuasion, only   235
Professes to persuade — the King his son's alive,
'Tis as impossible that he's undrown'd
As he that sleeps here swims.

Seb.   I have no hope
That he's undrown'd.

Ant.   O, out of that no hope
What great hope have you!   No hope that way is
Another way so high a hope that even   241
Ambition cannot pierce a wink beyond,
But doubt discovery there.   Will you grant with
      me
That Ferdinand is drown'd?

Seb.   He's gone.

Ant.   Then, tell me,
Who's the next heir of Naples?

Seb.   Claribel.   245

Ant. She that is Queen of Tunis; she that dwells
Ten leagues beyond man's life; she that from
      Naples
Can have no note, unless the sun were post —
The man i' the moon's too slow — till new-born
      chins   249
Be rough and razorable; she that — from whom
We all were sea-swallow'd, though some cast again,
And by that destiny to perform an act
Whereof what's past is prologue, what to come
In yours and my discharge.

Seb.   What stuff is this !   How say you ?
'Tis true, my brother's daughter's Queen of Tunis ;
So is she heir of Naples ;   'twixt which regions   256
There is some space.

Ant.   A space whose every cubit
Seems to cry out, "How shall that Claribel
Measure us back to Naples ?   Keep in Tunis,
And let Sebastian wake."   Say, this were death   260
That now hath seiz'd them ;   why, they were no
     worse
Than now they are.   There be that can rule Naples
As well as he that sleeps ;   lords that can prate
As amply and unnecessarily
As this Gonzalo ;   I myself could make   265
A chough of as deep chat.   O, that you bore
The mind that I do !   what a sleep were this
For your advancement !   Do you understand me ?

Seb. Methinks I do.

Ant.   And how does your content
Tender your own good fortune ?

Seb.   I remember   270
You did supplant your brother Prospero.

Ant.   True.
And look how well my garments sit upon me ;
Much feater than before.   My brother's servants
Were then my fellows ;   now they are my men.

Seb. But, for your conscience ?   275

Ant. Ay, sir, where lies that ?   If 'twere a kibe,

'Twould put me to my slipper ; but I feel not
This deity in my bosom.   Twenty consciences,
That stand 'twixt me and Milan, candied be they
And melt ere they molest !   Here lies your brother,
No better than the earth he lies upon   281
If he were that which now he's like, that's dead ;
Whom I, with this obedient steel, three inches of it,
Can lay to bed for ever ; whiles you, doing thus,
To the perpetual wink for aye might put   285
This ancient morsel, this Sir Prudence, who
Should not upbraid our course.   For all the rest,
They'll take suggestion as a cat laps milk ;
They'll tell the clock to any business that   289
We say befits the hour.

Seb.   Thy case, dear friend,
Shall be my precedent ; as thou got'st Milan,
I'll come by Naples.   Draw thy sword. One stroke
Shall free thee from the tribute which thou payest,
And I the King shall love thee.

Ant.   Draw together ;
And when I rear my hand, do you the like,   295
To fall it on Gonzalo.

Seb.   O, but one word.
                        [They talk apart.]

Re-enter Ariel [invisible], with music and song.

Ari. My master through his art foresees the danger
That you, his friend, are in ; and sends me forth —

For else his project dies — to keep them living.
Sings in Gonzalo's ear.

    While you here do snoring lie,   300
    Open-ey'd Conspiracy
        His time doth take.
    If of life you keep a care,
    Shake off slumber, and beware ;
        Awake, awake !   305

Ant. Then let us both be sudden.
Gon.   Now, good angels
    Preserve the King.   *[Wakes Alon.]*
Alon. Why, how now ? Ho, awake ! Why are you
    drawn ?
    Wherefore this ghastly looking ?
Gon.   What's the matter ?
Seb. Whiles we stood here securing your repose,   310
    Even now, we heard a hollow burst of bellowing
    Like bulls, or rather lions. Did't not wake you ?
    It struck mine ear most terribly.
Alon.   I heard nothing.
Ant. O, 'twas a din to fright a monster's ear,   314
    To make an earthquake ! Sure, it was the roar
    Of a whole herd of lions.
Alon.   Heard you this, Gonzalo ?
Gon. Upon mine honour, sir, I heard a humming,
    And that a strange one too, which did awake me.
    I shak'd you, sir, and cried. As mine eyes open'd,

I saw their weapons drawn. There was a noise,
That's verily. 'Tis best we stand upon our
    guard, 321
Or that we quit this place. Let's draw our
    weapons.

Alon. Lead off this ground; and let's make further
    search
For my poor son.

Gon.   Heavens keep him from these beasts!
For he is, sure, i' the island.

Alon.   Lead away. 325

Ari. Prospero my lord shall know what I have done.
So, King, go safely on to seek thy son. *Exeunt.*

SCENE II

[Another part of the island.]

*Enter Caliban with a burden of wood. A noise of
thunder heard.*

Cal. All the infections that the sun sucks up
From bogs, fens, flats, on Prosper fall and make
    him
By inch-meal a disease! His spirits hear me
And yet I needs must curse. But they'll nor
    pinch,
Fright me with urchin-shows, pitch me i' the mire,
Nor lead me, like a firebrand, in the dark 6

Out of my way, unless he bid 'em ; but
For every trifle are they set upon me,
Sometime like apes that mow and chatter at me
And after bite me, then like hedgehogs which   10
Lie tumbling in my barefoot way and mount
Their pricks at my footfall ; sometime am I
All wound with adders who with cloven tongues
Do hiss me into madness.

Enter Trinculo.

             Lo, now, lo !
Here comes a spirit of his, and to torment me   15
For bringing wood in slowly. I'll fall flat ;
Perchance he will not mind me.

Trin. Here's neither bush nor shrub, to bear off
any weather at all, and another storm brewing ;
I hear it sing i' the wind. Yond same black   20
cloud, yond huge one, looks like a foul bombard that would shed his liquor. If it should
thunder as it did before, I know not where to
hide my head ; yond same cloud cannot choose
but fall by pailfuls. What have we here ? A   25
man or a fish ? Dead or alive ? A fish ; he
smells like a fish ; a very ancient and fish-like
smell ; a kind of not-of-the-newest Poor-John.
A strange fish ! Were I in England now, as once
I was, and had but this fish painted, not a holiday fool there but would give a piece of silver.   30

There would this monster make a man; any
strange beast there makes a man. When they
will not give a doit to relieve a lame beggar, they
will lay out ten to see a dead Indian. Legg'd
like a man! and his fins like arms! Warm, o'my 35
troth! I do now let loose my opinion, hold it no
longer: this is no fish, but an islander, that hath
lately suffered by a thunderbolt. [*Thunder.*]
Alas, the storm is come again! My best way
is to creep under his gaberdine; there is no 40
other shelter hereabout. Misery acquaints
a man with strange bedfellows. I will here
shroud till the dregs of the storm be past.

Enter Stephano, singing: [a bottle in his hand].

Ste.   "I shall no more to sea, to sea,
           Here shall I die ashore —"   45

This is a very scurvy tune to sing at a man's
funeral. Well, here's my comfort.   *Drinks.*

(*Sings.*) "The master, the swabber, the boatswain,
       and I,
     The gunner and his mate
Lov'd Moll, Meg, and Marian, and Margery,   50
     But none of us car'd for Kate;
     For she had a tongue with a tang,
     Would cry to a sailor, Go hang!
She lov'd not the savour of tar nor of pitch,

Yet a tailor might scratch her where'er she did
    itch;   55
    Then to sea, boys, and let her go hang!"

This is a scurvy tune too; but here's my comfort.   *Drinks.*

Cal. Do not torment me! Oh!

Ste. What's the matter? Have we devils here? Do
you put tricks upon's with savages and men of   60
Ind, ha? I have not scap'd drowning to be
afeard now of your four legs; for it hath been
said, "As proper a man as ever went on four
legs cannot make him give ground"; and it
shall be said so again while Stephano breathes   65
at nostrils.

Cal. The spirit torments me! Oh!

Ste. This is some monster of the isle with four
legs, who hath got, as I take it, an ague.
Where the devil should he learn our language?
I will give him some relief, if it be but for   70
that. If I can recover him and keep him tame
and get to Naples with him, he's a present for
any emperor that ever trod on neat's-leather.

Cal. Do not torment me, prithee; I'll bring my
wood home faster.   75

Ste. He's in his fit now and does not talk after the
wisest. He shall taste of my bottle; if he have
never drunk wine afore, it will go near to re-

E

move his fit. If I can recover him and keep
him tame, I will not take too much for him; he 80
shall pay for him that hath him, and that
soundly.

Cal. Thou dost me yet but little hurt; thou wilt
anon, I know it by thy trembling. Now
Prosper works upon thee.

Ste. Come on your ways. Open your mouth; here 85
is that which will give language to you, cat.
Open your mouth; this will shake your shaking,
I can tell you, and that soundly. You cannot
tell who's your friend. Open your chaps again.

Trin. I should know that voice; it should be 90
— but he is drown'd; and these are devils.
O defend me!

Ste. Four legs and two voices; a most delicate
monster! His forward voice now is to speak
well of his friend; his backward voice is to 95
utter foul speeches and to detract. If all the
wine in my bottle will recover him, I will help
his ague. Come. Amen! I will pour some in
thy other mouth.

Trin. Stephano! 100

Ste. Doth thy other mouth call me? Mercy,
mercy! This is a devil, and no monster. I
will leave him; I have no long spoon.

Trin. Stephano! If thou beest Stephano, touch
me and speak to me; for I am Trinculo, — 105
be not afeard — thy good friend Trinculo.

Ste. If thou beest Trinculo, come forth. I'll pull
    thee by the lesser legs. If any be Trinculo's
    legs, these are they. Thou art very Trinculo
    indeed! How cam'st thou to be the siege of   110
    this moon-calf? Can he vent Trinculos?

Trin. I took him to be kill'd with a thunderstroke.
    But art thou not drown'd, Stephano? I hope
    now thou art not drown'd. Is the storm over-
    blown? I hid me under the dead moon-calf's   115
    gaberdine for fear of the storm. And art thou
    living, Stephano? O Stephano, two Neapoli-
    tans scap'd!

Ste. Prithee, do not turn me about; my stomach
    is not constant.

Cal. [*Aside.*] These be fine things, an if they be not
        sprites.   120
    That's a brave god and bears celestial liquor.
    I will kneel to him.

Ste. How didst thou scape? How cam'st thou
    hither? Swear by this bottle how thou
    cam'st hither, — I escap'd upon a butt of sack   125
    which the sailors heaved o'erboard — by this
    bottle, which I made of the bark of a tree with
    mine own hands since I was cast ashore.

Cal. I'll swear upon that bottle to be thy true
    subject; for the liquor is not earthly.   130

Ste. Here; swear then how thou escap'dst.

Trin. Swam ashore, man, like a duck. I can
    swim like a duck, I'll be sworn,

Ste. Here, kiss the book. Though thou canst
    swim like a duck, thou art made like a goose. 135
Trin. O Stephano, hast any more of this?
Ste. The whole butt, man. My cellar is in a
    rock by the seaside where my wine is hid.
    How now, moon-calf! how does thine ague?
Cal. Hast thou not dropp'd from heaven?   140
Ste. Out o' the moon, I do assure thee. I was
    the man i' the moon when time was.
Cal. I have seen thee in her and I do adore thee.
    My mistress show'd me thee and thy dog and thy
        bush.
Ste. Come, swear to that; kiss the book. I will 145
    furnish it anon with new contents. Swear.
Trin. By this good light, this is a very shallow mon-
    ster! I afeard of him! A very weak monster!
    The man i' the moon! A most poor credulous
    monster! Well drawn, monster, in good sooth! 150
Cal. I'll show thee every fertile inch o' the island;
    And I will kiss thy foot. I prithee, be my god.
Trin. By this light, a most perfidious and drunken
    monster! When's god's asleep, he'll rob
    his bottle.   155
Cal. I'll kiss thy foot. I'll swear myself thy subject.
Ste. Come on then; down, and swear.
Trin. I shall laugh myself to death at this puppy-
    headed monster. A most scurvy monster!
    I could find in my heart to beat him —   160

Ste. Come, kiss.

Trin. But that the poor monster's in drink. An
     abominable monster!

Cal. I'll show thee the best springs; I'll pluck thee
        berries;

     I'll fish for thee and get thee wood enough. 165
     A plague upon the tyrant that I serve!
     I'll bear him no more sticks, but follow thee,
     Thou wondrous man.

Trin. A most ridiculous monster, to make a won-
     der of a poor drunkard!   170

Cal. I prithee, let me bring thee where crabs grow;
     And I with my long nails will dig thee pig-
        nuts;
     Show thee a jay's nest and instruct thee how
     To snare the nimble marmoset. I'll bring thee
     To clust'ring filberts and sometimes I'll get
        thee   175
     Young scamels from the rock. Wilt thou go with
        me?

Ste. I prithee now, lead the way without any
     more talking. Trinculo, the King and all our
     company else being drown'd, we will in-
     herit here. Here! bear my bottle. Fellow 180
     Trinculo, we'll fill him by and by again.

Cal. (*Sings drunkenly.*)
        Farewell, master; farewell, farewell!

Trin. A howling monster; a drunken monster!

Cal. No more dams I'll make for fish;
         Nor fetch in firing   185
         At requiring;
  Nor scrape trenchering, nor wash dish.
      'Ban, 'Ban, Cacaliban
      Has a new master, get a new man.
  Freedom, hey-day! hey-day, freedom! free-   190
dom, hey-day, freedom!

Ste. O brave monster! Lead the way.   *Exeunt.*

ACT THIRD

SCENE I

[Before Prospero's cell.]

Enter Ferdinand, bearing a log.

Fer. There be some sports are painful, and their labour
    Delight in them sets off; some kinds of baseness
    Are nobly undergone, and most poor matters
    Point to rich ends. This my mean task
    Would be as heavy to me as odious, but   5
    The mistress which I serve quickens what's dead
    And makes my labours pleasures. O, she is
    Ten times more gentle than her father's crabbed,
    And he's compos'd of harshness. I must remove
    Some thousands of these logs and pile them up, 10
    Upon a sore injunction. My sweet mistress
    Weeps when she sees me work, and says such baseness
    Had never like executor. I forget;
    But these sweet thoughts do even refresh my labours,   14
    Most busy least, when I do it.

Enter Miranda; and Prospero [at a distance, unseen].

Mir.   Alas, now, pray you,
Work not so hard. I would the lightning had
Burnt up those logs that you are enjoin'd to
    pile !
Pray, set it down and rest you. When this
    burns,
'Twill weep for having wearied you. My
    father
Is hard at study; pray now, rest yourself;   20
He's safe for these three hours.

Fer.   O most dear mistress,
The sun will set before I shall discharge
What I must strive to do.

Mir.   If you'll sit down,
I'll bear your logs the while. Pray, give me
    that ;
                                24
I'll carry it to the pile.

Fer.   No, precious creature ;
I had rather crack my sinews, break my back,
Than you should such dishonour undergo,
While I sit lazy by.

Mir.   It would become me
As well as it does you ; and I should do it
With much more ease, for my good will is to
    it,
                                30
And yours it is against.

Pros.   Poor worm, thou art infected !
     This visitation shows it.

Mir.   You look wearily.

Fer. No, noble mistress; 'tis fresh morning with
     me
     When you are by at night.   I do beseech you —
     Chiefly that I might set it in my prayers —   35
     What is your name ?

Mir.   Miranda. — O my father,
     I have broke your hest to say so !

Fer.   Admir'd Miranda !
     Indeed the top of admiration ! worth
     What's dearest to the world !   Full many a lady
     I have ey'd with best regard, and many a
     time   40
     The harmony of their tongues hath into bond-
     age
     Brought my too diligent ear; for several vir-
     tues
     Have I lik'd several women, never any
     With so full soul, but some defect in her
     Did quarrel with the noblest grace she ow'd   45
     And put it to the foil; but you, O you,
     So perfect and so peerless, are created
     Of every creature's best !

Mir.   I do not know
     One of my sex; no woman's face remember,
     Save, from my glass, mine own; nor have I seen

More that I may call men than you, good friend,   51
And my dear father. How features are abroad,
I am skilless of; but, by my modesty,
The jewel in my dower, I would not wish
Any companion in the world but you,   55
Nor can imagination form a shape,
Besides yourself, to like of. But I prattle
Something too wildly, and my father's precepts
I therein do forget.

Fer.   I am in my condition
A prince, Miranda; I do think, a king;   60
I would, not so! — and would no more endure
This wooden slavery than to suffer
The flesh-fly blow my mouth. Hear my soul
     speak.
The very instant that I saw you, did
My heart fly to your service; there resides,   65
To make me slave to it; and for your sake
Am I this patient log-man.

Mir.   Do you love me?

Fer. O heaven, O earth, bear witness to this sound,
And crown what I profess with kind event
If I speak true! if hollowly, invert   70
What best is boded me to mischief! I
Beyond all limit of what else i' the world
Do love, prize, honour you.

Mir.   I am a fool
To weep at what I am glad of.

Pros.   Fair encounter
    Of two most rare affections! Heavens rain
      grace   75
    On that which breeds between 'em!
Fer.   Wherefore weep you?
Mir. At mine unworthiness, that dare not offer
    What I desire to give, and much less take
    What I shall die to want. But this is trifling;
    And all the more it seeks to hide itself,   80
    The bigger bulk it shows. Hence, bashful cunning!
    And prompt me, plain and holy innocence!
    I am your wife, if you will marry me;
    If not, I'll die your maid. To be your fellow
    You may deny me; but I'll be your servant, 85
    Whether you will or no.
Fer.   My mistress, dearest;
    And I thus humble ever.
Mir.   My husband, then?
Fer. Ay, with a heart as willing
    As bondage e'er of freedom. Here's my hand.
Mir. And mine, with my heart in't. And now fare-
      well   90
    Till half an hour hence.
Fer.   A thousand thousand!
      Exeunt [Fer. and Mir. severally].
Pros. So glad of this as they I cannot be,
    Who are surpris'd withal; but my rejoicing
    At nothing can be more. I'll to my book,

For yet ere supper-time must I perform   95
Much business appertaining.   *Exit.*

SCENE II

[Another part of the island.]

Enter Caliban, Stephano, and Trinculo.

Ste. Tell not me. When the butt is out, we will
drink water; not a drop before; therefore
bear up, and board 'em. Servant-monster,
drink to me.

Trin. Servant-monster! the folly of this island!   5
They say there's but five upon this isle:
we are three of them; if the other two be
brain'd like us, the state totters.

Ste. Drink, servant-monster, when I bid thee.
Thy eyes are almost set in thy head.   10

Trin. Where should they be set else? He were
a brave monster indeed, if they were set in
his tail.

Ste. My man-monster hath drown'd his tongue in
sack. For my part, the sea cannot drown me;   15
I swam, ere I could recover the shore, five and
thirty leagues off and on. By this light, thou
shalt be my lieutenant, monster, or my standard.

Trin. Your lieutenant, if you list; he's no standard.   20

Ste. We'll not run, Monsieur Monster.

Trin. Nor go neither; but you'll lie like dogs
and yet say nothing neither.

Ste. Moon-calf, speak once in thy life, if thou
beest a good moon-calf.   25

Cal. How does thy honour? Let me lick thy shoe.
I'll not serve him; he's not valiant.

Trin. Thou liest, most ignorant monster! I am
in case to justle a constable. Why, thou debosh'd fish, thou, was there ever man a cow-   30
ard that hath drunk so much sack as I to-day?
Wilt thou tell a monstrous lie, being but half
a fish and half a monster?

Cal. Lo, how he mocks me! Wilt thou let him,
my lord?   35

Trin. "Lord" quoth he! That a monster should
be such a natural!

Cal. Lo, lo, again! Bite him to death, I
prithee.

Ste. Trinculo, keep a good tongue in your head.
If you prove a mutineer, — the next tree!   40
The poor monster's my subject and he shall
not suffer indignity.

Cal. I thank my noble lord. Wilt thou be pleas'd
to hearken once again to the suit I made to
thee?   45

Ste. Marry, will I; kneel and repeat it. I
will stand, and so shall Trinculo.

Enter Ariel, invisible.

Cal. As I told thee before, I am subject to a
tyrant, a sorcerer, that by his cunning hath
cheated me of the island.   50

Ari. Thou liest.

Cal. Thou liest, thou jesting monkey, thou.
I would my valiant master would destroy
thee! I do not lie.

Ste. Trinculo, if you trouble him any more   55
in's tale, by this hand, I will supplant some of
your teeth.

Trin. Why, I said nothing.

Ste. Mum, then, and no more. Proceed.

Cal. I say, by sorcery he got this isle;   60
From me he got it. If thy greatness will
Revenge it on him, — for I know thou dar'st,
But this thing dare not, —

Ste. That's most certain.

Cal. Thou shalt be lord of it and I'll serve thee.   65

Ste. How now shall this be compass'd? Canst
thou bring me to the party?

Cal. Yea, yea, my lord. I'll yield him thee asleep,
Where thou mayst knock a nail into his head.

Ari. Thou liest; thou canst not.   70

Cal. What a pied ninny's this! Thou scurvy patch!
I do beseech thy greatness, give him blows
And take his bottle from him. When that's gone

He shall drink nought but brine; for I'll not
    show him
Where the quick freshes are.   75

Ste. Trinculo, run into no further danger. In-
    terrupt the monster one word further, and,
    by this hand, I'll turn my mercy out o' doors
    and make a stock-fish of thee.

Trin. Why, what did I? I did nothing. I'll go 80
    farther off.

Ste. Didst thou not say he lied?

Ari. Thou liest.

Ste. Do I so? Take thou that. [*Beats Trin.*] As
    you like this, give me the lie another time.   85

Trin. I did not give the lie. Out o' your wits
    and hearing too? A pox o' your bottle! this
    can sack and drinking do. A murrain on your
    monster, and the devil take your fingers!

Cal. Ha, ha, ha!   90

Ste. Now, forward with your tale. Prithee,
    stand farther off.

Cal. Beat him enough. After a little time
    I'll beat him too.

Ste.   Stand farther. Come, proceed.

Cal. Why, as I told thee, 'tis a custom with him,   95
    I' the afternoon to sleep. There thou mayst
        brain him,
Having first seiz'd his books, or with a log
Batter his skull, or paunch him with a stake,

Or cut his wezand with thy knife. Remember
First to possess his books; for without them 100
He's but a sot, as I am, nor hath not
One spirit to command. They all do hate him
As rootedly as I. Burn but his books.
He has brave utensils, — for so he calls them, —
Which, when he has a house, he'll deck withal.
And that most deeply to consider is   106
The beauty of his daughter. He himself
Calls her a nonpareil. I never saw a woman
But only Sycorax my dam and she;
But she as far surpasseth Sycorax   110
As greatest does least.

Ste.   Is it so brave a lass?

Cal. Ay, lord; she will become thy bed, I warrant,
And bring thee forth brave brood.

Ste. Monster, I will kill this man. His daughter
and I will be king and queen, — save our 115
Graces! — and Trinculo and thyself shall be
viceroys. Dost thou like the plot, Trinculo?

Trin. Excellent.

Ste. Give me thy hand. I am sorry I beat thee;
but, while thou liv'st, keep a good tongue 120
in thy head.

Cal. Within this half hour will he be asleep.
Wilt thou destroy him then?

Ste.   Ay, on mine honour.

Ari. This will I tell my master.

Cal. Thou mak'st me merry; I am full of pleas-
     ure.   125
     Let us be jocund. Will you troll the catch
     You taught me but while-ere?

Ste. At thy request, monster, I will do reason,
     any reason. Come on, Trinculo, let us sing.

Sings.

         Flout 'em and scout 'em   130
         And scout 'em and flout 'em;
           Thought is free.

Cal. That's not the tune.

         Ariel plays the tune on a tabor and pipe.

Ste. What is this same?

Trin. This is the tune of our catch, played by   135
     the picture of Nobody.

Ste. If thou beest a man, show thyself in thy like-
     ness. If thou be'st a devil, take't as thou list.

Trin. O, forgive me my sins!

Ste. He that dies pays all debts. I defy thee.   140
     Mercy upon us!

Cal. Art thou afeard?

Ste. No, monster, not I.

Cal. Be not afeard. The isle is full of noises,
     Sounds and sweet airs, that give delight and
         hurt not.   145
     Sometimes a thousand twangling instruments
     Will hum about mine ears, and sometime voices
     That, if I then had wak'd after long sleep,

F

Will make me sleep again; and then, in dreaming,
The clouds methought would open and show
    riches   150
Ready to drop upon me, that, when I wak'd,
I cried to dream again.

Ste. This will prove a brave kingdom to me, where
    I shall have my music for nothing.

Cal. When Prospero is destroy'd.   155

Ste. That shall be by and by. I remember the story.

Trin. The sound is going away. Let's follow it,
    and after do our work.

Ste. Lead, monster; we'll follow. I would I
    could see this taborer; he lays it on.   160

Trin. Wilt come? I'll follow, Stephano.   *Exeunt.*

SCENE III

[Another part of the island.]

*Enter Alonso, Sebastian, Antonio, Gonzalo, Adrian,
Francisco, etc.*

Gon. By'r lakin, I can go no further, sir;
    My old bones ache. Here's a maze trod indeed
    Through forth-rights and meanders! By your
        patience,
    I needs must rest me.

Alon.   Old lord, I cannot blame thee,
    Who am myself attach'd with weariness   5

To the dulling of my spirits. Sit down, and rest.
Even here I will put off my hope and keep it
No longer for my flatterer. He is drown'd
Whom thus we stray to find, and the sea mocks
Our frustrate search on land. Well, let him
  go.   10

Ant. [*Aside to Seb.*] I am right glad that he's so
  out of hope.
Do not, for one repulse, forego the purpose
That you resolv'd to effect.

Seb.   [*Aside to Ant.*] The next advantage
Will we take throughly.

Ant.   [*Aside to Seb.*] Let it be to-night ;
For, now they are oppress'd with travel, they 15
Will not, nor cannot, use such vigilance
As when they are fresh.

*Solemn and strange music ; and Prospero on the top
 invisible. Enter several strange shapes, bringing in
 a banquet ; and dance about it with gentle actions of
 salutation ; and, inviting the King, etc., to eat, they
 depart.*

Seb.   [*Aside to Ant.*] I say, to-night. No more.

Alon. What harmony is this ? My good friends,
  hark !

Gon. Marvellous sweet music !

Alon. Give us kind keepers, heavens ! What were
  these ?   20

Seb. A living drollery. Now I will believe
 That there are unicorns, that in Arabia
 There is one tree, the phœnix' throne, one phœnix
 At this hour reigning there.

Ant.   I'll believe both :
 And what does else want credit, come to me, 25
 And I'll be sworn 'tis true. Travellers ne'er
  did lie,
 Though fools at home condemn 'em.

Gon.   If in Naples
 I should report this now, would they believe
  me ?
 If I should say, I saw such islanders —
 For, certes, these are people of the island —   30
 Who, though they are of monstrous shape, yet,
  note,
 Their manners are more gentle, kind, than of
 Our human generation you shall find
 Many, nay, almost any.

Pros.   [*Aside.*] Honest lord,
 Thou hast said well ; for some of you there
  present   35
 Are worse than devils.

Alon.   I cannot too much muse
 Such shapes, such gesture, and such sound, ex-
  pressing,
 Although they want the use of tongue, a kind
 Of excellent dumb discourse.

Pros.   [*Aside.*] Praise in departing.

Fran. They vanish'd strangely.

Seb.   No matter, since
    They have left their viands behind, for we have
       stomachs.   41
    Will't please you taste of what is here?

Alon.   Not I.

Gon. Faith, sir, you need not fear. When we were
      boys,
    Who would believe that there were mountain-
      eers
    Dew-lapp'd like bulls, whose throats had hanging
      at 'em   45
    Wallets of flesh? or that there were such men
    Whose heads stood in their breasts? which now
      we find
    Each putter-out of five for one will bring us
    Good warrant of.

Alon.   I will stand to and feed,
    Although my last. No matter, since I feel   50
    The best is past. Brother, my lord the Duke,
    Stand to and do as we.

*Thunder and lightning. Enter Ariel, like a harpy;
claps his wings upon the table; and, with a quaint
device, the banquet vanishes.*

Ari. You are three men of sin, whom Destiny,
    That hath to instrument this lower world

And what is in't, the never-surfeited sea   55
Hath caus'd to belch up you; and on this
      island
Where man doth not inhabit; you 'mongst men
Being most unfit to live. I have made you mad;
And even with such-like valour men hang and
      drown
Their proper selves.

          [*Alon., Seb., etc., draw their swords.*]
               You fools ! I and my fellows
Are ministers of Fate. The elements,   61
Of whom your swords are temper'd, may as well
Wound the loud winds, or with bemock'd-at
      stabs
Kill the still-closing waters, as diminish
One dowle that's in my plume. My fellow-
      ministers   65
Are like invulnerable. If you could hurt,
Your swords are now too massy for your
      strengths
And will not be uplifted. But remember —
For that's my business to you — that you three
From Milan did supplant good Prospero;   70
Expos'd unto the sea, which hath requit it,
Him and his innocent child; for which foul deed
The powers, delaying, not forgetting, have
Incens'd the seas and shores, yea, all the crea-
      tures,

Against your peace.   Thee of thy son, Alonso, 75
They have bereft; and do pronounce by me
Ling'ring perdition, worse than any death
Can be at once, shall step by step attend
You and your ways; whose wraths to guard
     you from —
Which here, in this most desolate isle, else falls   80
Upon your heads — is nothing but heart's sorrow
And a clear life ensuing.

He vanishes in thunder; then, to soft music, enter the
*   shapes again, and dance, with mocks and mows,*
*   and carrying out the table.*

Pros.   Bravely the figure of this harpy hast thou
     Perform'd, my Ariel; a grace it had, devouring.
     Of my instruction hast thou nothing bated   85
     In what thou hadst to say; so, with good life
     And observation strange, my meaner ministers
     Their several kinds have done.   My high charms
         work,
     And these mine enemies are all knit up
     In their distractions.   They now are in my
         power;   90
     And in these fits I leave them, while I visit
     Young Ferdinand, whom they suppose is
         drown'd,
     And his and mine lov'd darling.   *[Exit above.]*

Gon. I' the name of something holy, sir, why stand
    you
    In this strange stare?
Alon.   O, it is monstrous, monstrous!
    Methought the billows spoke and told me of it;
    The winds did sing it to me, and the thunder,   97
    That deep and dreadful organ-pipe, pronounc'd
    The name of Prosper; it did bass my trespass.
    Therefore my son i' the ooze is bedded, and   100
    I'll seek him deeper than e'er plummet sounded
    And with him there lie mudded.   *[Exit.]*
Seb.   But one fiend at a time,
    I'll fight their legions o'er.
Ant.   I'll be thy second.
                   Exeunt [Seb. and Ant.].
Gon. All three of them are desperate: their great
    guilt,   104
    Like poison given to work a great time after,
    Now gins to bite the spirits. I do beseech you
    That are of suppler joints, follow them swiftly
    And hinder them from what this ecstasy
    May now provoke them to.
Adr.   Follow, I pray you.
                              Exeunt.

ACT FOURTH

SCENE I

[Before Prospero's cell.]

Enter Prospero, Ferdinand, and Miranda.

Pros. If I have too austerely punish'd you,
    Your compensation makes amends, for I
    Have given you here a third of mine own life,
    Or that for which I live ; who once again
    I tender to thy hand. All thy vexations   5
    Were but my trials of thy love, and thou
    Hast strangely stood the test. Here, afore Heaven,
    I ratify this my rich gift. O Ferdinand,
    Do not smile at me that I boast her off,
    For thou shalt find she will outstrip all praise   10
    And make it halt behind her.
Fer.   I do believe it
    Against an oracle.
Pros.   Then, as my gift and thine own acquisition
    Worthily purchas'd, take my daughter. But
    If thou dost break her virgin-knot before   15
    All sanctimonious ceremonies may
    With full and holy rite be minist'red,
    No sweet aspersion shall the heavens let fall
    To make this contract grow ; but barren Hate,

Sour-eyed Disdain and Discord shall bestrew   20
The union of your bed with weeds so loathly
That you shall hate it both.   Therefore take heed,
As Hymen's lamps shall light you.

Fer.   As I hope
For quiet days, fair issue, and long life,
With such love as 'tis now, the murkiest den,   25
The most opportune place, the strong'st suggestion
Our worser genius can, shall never melt
Mine honour into lust, to take away
The edge of that day's celebration
When I shall think or Phœbus' steeds are foun-
     der'd   30
Or Night kept chain'd below.

Pros.   Fairly spoke.
Sit then and talk with her ; she is thine own.
What, Ariel ! my industrious servant, Ariel !

Enter Ariel.

Ari. What would my potent master ?   Here I am.
Pros. Thou and thy meaner fellows your last service
Did worthily perform ; and I must use you   36
In such another trick.   Go bring the rabble,
O'er whom I give thee power, here to this place.
Incite them to quick motion ; for I must
Bestow upon the eyes of this young couple   40
Some vanity of mine art.   It is my promise,
And they expect it from me.

Ari.   Presently ?

Pros. Ay, with a twink.

Ari. Before you can say "come" and "go,"

And breathe twice and cry "so, so,"   45

Each one, tripping on his toe,

Will be here with mop and mow.

Do you love me, master ?   No ?

Pros. Dearly, my delicate Ariel.   Do not approach

Till thou dost hear me call.

Ari.   Well, I conceive.   50

                                        Exit.

Pros. Look thou be true ; do not give dalliance

Too much the rein.   The strongest oaths are straw

To the fire i' the blood.   Be more abstemious,

Or else, good night your vow !

Fer.   I warrant you, sir ;

The white cold virgin snow upon my heart   55

Abates the ardour of my liver.

Pros.   Well.

Now come, my Ariel ! bring a corollary,

Rather than want a spirit.   Appear, and pertly !

No tongue ! all eyes ! Be silent.   *Soft music.*

Enter Iris.

Iris. Ceres, most bounteous lady, thy rich leas   60

Of wheat, rye, barley, vetches, oats, and pease ;

Thy turfy mountains, where live nibbling sheep,

And flat meads thatch'd with stover, them to keep :

Thy banks with pioned and twilled brims,
Which spongy April at thy hest betrims   65
To make cold nymphs chaste crowns; and thy
    brown groves,
Whose shadow the dismissed bachelor loves,
Being lass-lorn; thy pole-clipp'd vineyard;
And thy sea-marge, sterile and rocky-hard,
Where thou thyself dost air;—the queen o' the
    sky,   70
Whose watery arch and messenger am I,
Bids thee leave these, and with her sovereign grace,
                Juno descends.

Here on this grass-plot, in this very place,
To come and sport; here peacocks fly amain.
Approach, rich Ceres, her to entertain.   75

Enter Ceres.

Cer. Hail, many-coloured messenger, that ne'er
    Dost disobey the wife of Jupiter;
    Who with thy saffron wings upon my flowers
    Diffusest honey-drops, refreshing showers,
    And with each end of thy blue bow dost crown   80
    My bosky acres and my unshrubb'd down,
    Rich scarf to my proud earth; why hath thy queen
    Summon'd me hither, to this short-grass'd green?

Iris. A contract of true love to celebrate;
    And some donation freely to estate   85
    On the blest lovers.

Cer.   Tell me, heavenly bow,
     If Venus or her son, as thou dost know,
     Do now attend the Queen ?   Since they did plot
     The means that dusky Dis my daughter got,
     Her and her blind boy's scandal'd company   90
     I have forsworn.

Iris.   Of her society
     Be not afraid.   I met her deity
     Cutting the clouds towards Paphos, and her son
     Dove-drawn with her.   Here thought they to have done
     Some wanton charm upon this man and maid,   95
     Whose vows are, that no bed-right shall be paid
     Till Hymen's torch be lighted ; but in vain.
     Mars's hot minion is return'd again ;
     Her waspish-headed son has broke his arrows,
     Swears he will shoot no more, but play with spar-
         rows   100
     And be a boy right out.

Cer.   Highest queen of **state,**
     Great Juno, comes ; I know her by her gait.

                 [*Enter Juno.*]

Juno.   How does my bounteous sister ?   Go with me
     To bless this twain, that they may prosperous be
     And honour'd in their issue.   *They sing.*

Juno.   Honour, riches, marriage-blessing,   106
     Long continuance, and increasing,

Hourly joys be still upon you !
Juno sings her blessings on you.

[*Cer.*]   Earth's increase, foison plenty,   110
Barns and garners never empty,
Vines with clustering bunches growing,
Plants with goodly burden bowing.
Spring come to you at the farthest
In the very end of harvest !   115
Scarcity and want shall shun you ;
Ceres' blessing so is on you.

Fer.   This is a most majestic vision, and
Harmonious charmingly.   May I be bold
To think these spirits ?

Pros.   Spirits, which by mine art
I have from their confines call'd to enact   121
My present fancies.

Fer.   Let me live here ever ;
So rare a wond'red father and a wise
Makes this place Paradise.

Pros.   Sweet, now, silence !
Juno and Ceres whisper seriously.   125
There's something else to do ; hush, and be mute,
Or else our spell is marr'd.

>   *Juno and Ceres whisper, and send Iris on*
>   *employment.*

Iris. You nymphs, call'd Naiads, of the winding
brooks,
With your sedg'd crowns and ever-harmless looks,

Leave your crisp channels, and on this green land
Answer your summons; Juno does command.   131
Come, temperate nymphs, and help to celebrate
A contract of true love; be not too late.

Enter certain Nymphs.

You sunburnt sicklemen, of August weary,
Come hither from the furrow and be merry.   135
Make holiday; your rye-straw hats put on
And these fresh nymphs encounter every one
In country footing.

Enter certain Reapers, properly habited: they join with
the Nymphs in a graceful dance; towards the end
whereof Prospero starts suddenly, and speaks; after
which, to a strange, hollow, and confused noise, they
heavily vanish.

Pros. [*Aside.*] I had forgot that foul conspiracy
     Of the beast Caliban and his confederates   140
     Against my life. The minute of their plot
     Is almost come. [*To the Spirits.*] Well done! avoid.
       No more!
Fer. This is strange. Your father's in some passion
     That works him strongly.
Mir.   Never till this day
     Saw I him touch'd with anger, so distemper'd.   145
Pros. You do look, my son, in a mov'd sort,
     As if you were dismay'd. Be cheerful, sir,

Our revels now are ended.   These our actors,
As I foretold you, were all spirits, and
Are melted into air, into thin air;   150
And, like the baseless fabric of this vision,
The cloud-capp'd towers, the gorgeous palaces,
The solemn temples, the great globe itself,
Yea, all which it inherit, shall dissolve
And, like this insubstantial pageant faded,   155
Leave not a rack behind.   We are such stuff
As dreams are made on, and our little life
Is rounded with a sleep.   Sir, I am vex'd, —
Bear with my weakness — my old brain is troubled.
Be not disturb'd with my infirmity.   160
If you be pleas'd, retire into my cell
And there repose.   A turn or two I'll walk,
To still my beating mind.

Fer. Mir.   We wish your peace.
                                   Exeunt.

Pros. Come with a thought.   I thank thee, Ariel;
come.

Enter Ariel.

Ari. Thy thoughts I cleave to.   What's thy pleasure?
Pros.   Spirit,   165
We must prepare to meet with Caliban.

Ari. Ay, my commander.   When I presented Ceres,
I thought to have told thee of it, but I fear'd
Lest I might anger thee.   169

Pros. Say again, where didst thou leave these varlets?
Ari. I told you, sir, they were red-hot with drinking;
So full of valour that they smote the air
For breathing in their faces; beat the ground
For kissing of their feet; yet always bending
Towards their project. Then I beat my tabor;
At which, like unback'd colts, they prick'd their
       ears,   176
Advanc'd their eyelids, lifted up their noses
As they smelt music. So I charm'd their ears
That calf-like they my lowing follow'd through
Tooth'd briers, sharp furzes, pricking gorse, and
       thorns,   180
Which ent'red their frail shins. At last I left
     them
I' the filthy-mantled pool beyond your cell,
There dancing up to the chins, that the foul lake
O'erstunk their feet.
Pros.   This was well done, my bird.
Thy shape invisible retain thou still.   185
The trumpery in my house, go bring it hither,
For stale to catch these thieves.
Ari.   I go, I go.

                          Exit.

Pros. A devil, a born devil, on whose nature
Nurture can never stick; on whom my pains,
Humanely taken, all, all lost, quite lost;   190
And as with age his body uglier grows,

G

So his mind cankers.   I will plague them all,
Even to roaring.

Re-enter Ariel, loaden with glittering apparel, etc.

                  Come, hang them on this line.

[*Prospero and Ariel remain, invisible.*]   *Enter Caliban,
Stephano, and Trinculo, all wet.*

Cal. Pray you, tread softly, that the blind mole may
     not
    Hear a foot fall ; we now are near his cell.   195
Ste. Monster, your fairy, which you say is a harm-
    less fairy, has done little better than play'd the
    Jack with us.
Trin. Monster, I do smell all horse-piss, at which
    my nose is in great indignation.   200
Ste. So is mine. Do you hear, monster ? If I
    should take a displeasure against you, look
    you, —
Trin. Thou wert but a lost monster.
Cal. Good my lord, give me thy favour still.
    Be patient, for the prize I'll bring thee to   205
    Shall hoodwink this mischance ; therefore speak
     softly,
    All's hush'd as midnight yet.
Trin. Ay, but to lose our bottles in the pool, —
Ste. There is not only disgrace and dishonour in
    that, monster, but an infinite loss.   210

Trin. That's more to me than my wetting; yet
     this is your harmless fairy, monster !

Ste. I will fetch off my bottle, though I be o'er ears
     for my labour.

Cal. Prithee, my king, be quiet. See'st thou here, 215
     This is the mouth o' the cell. No noise, and enter.
     Do that good mischief which may make this island
     Thine own for ever, and I, thy Caliban,
     For aye thy foot-licker.

Ste. Give me thy hand. I do begin to have bloody 220
     thoughts.

Trin. O King Stephano ! O peer ! O worthy Ste-
     phano ! look what a wardrobe here is for thee !

Cal. Let it alone, thou fool ; it is but trash.

Trin. O, ho, monster ! we know what belongs to a 225
     frippery. O King Stephano !

Ste. Put off that gown, Trinculo ; by this hand,
     I'll have that gown.

Trin. Thy Grace shall have it.

Cal. The dropsy drown this fool ! what do you mean
     To dote thus on such luggage ? Let's alone   231
     And do the murder first. If he awake,
     From toe to crown he'll fill our skins with pinches,
     Make us strange stuff.

Ste. Be you quiet, monster. Mistress line, is not 235
     this my jerkin ? Now is the jerkin under the
     line. Now, jerkin, you are like to lose your
     hair and prove a bald jerkin.

Trin. Do, do; we steal by line and level, an't like
your Grace.   240

Ste. I thank thee for that jest; here's a garment
for't. Wit shall not go unrewarded while I am
king of this country. "Steal by line and
level" is an excellent pass of pate; there's
another garment for't.   245

Trin. Monster, come, put some lime upon your
fingers, and away with the rest.

Cal. I will have none on't. We shall lose our time,
And all be turn'd to barnacles, or to apes
With foreheads villanous low.   250

Ste. Monster, lay-to your fingers. Help to bear
this away where my hogshead of wine is, or I'll
turn you out of my kingdom. Go to, carry this.

Trin. And this.

Ste. Ay, and this.   255

*A noise of hunters heard. Enter divers Spirits, in shape
of dogs and hounds, hunting them about, Prospero
and Ariel setting them on.*

Pros. Hey, Mountain, hey!

Ari. Silver! there it goes, Silver!

Pros. Fury, Fury! there, Tyrant, there! hark! hark!
[*Cal., Ste., and Trin. are driven out.*]
Go charge my goblins that they grind their joints
With dry convulsions, shorten up their sinews

With aged cramps, and more pinch-spotted make
    them   261
Than pard or cat o' mountain.

Ari.   Hark, they roar !

Pros. Let them be hunted soundly. At this hour
Lies at my mercy all mine enemies.
Shortly shall all my labours end, and thou   265
Shalt have the air at freedom. For a little
Follow, and do me service.   *Exeunt.*

ACT FIFTH

Scene I

[Before Prospero's cell.]

Enter Prospero in his magic robes, and Ariel.

Pros. Now does my project gather to a head.
    My charms crack not; my spirits obey; and Time
    Goes upright with his carriage. How's the day?
Ari. On the sixth hour; at which time, my lord,
    You said our work should cease.
Pros.   I did say so, 5
    When first I rais'd the tempest. Say, my spirit,
    How fares the King and 's followers?
Ari.   Confin'd together
    In the same fashion as you gave in charge,
    Just as you left them; all prisoners, sir, 9
    In the line-grove which weather-fends your cell;
    They cannot budge till your release. The King
    His brother, and yours, abide all three distracted,
    And the remainder mourning over them,
    Brimful of sorrow and dismay; but chiefly
    Him that you term'd, sir, "The good old lord, Gonzalo," 15
    His tears run down his beard, like winter's drops

      From eaves of reeds. Your charm so strongly
          works 'em
      That if you now beheld them, your affections
      Would become tender.

Pros.   Dost thou think so, spirit?
Ari. Mine would, sir, were I human.
Pros.   And mine shall.
      Hast thou, which art but air, a touch, a feeling   21
      Of their afflictions, and shall not myself,
      One of their kind, that relish all as sharply
      Passion as they, be kindlier mov'd than thou art?
      Though with their high wrongs I am struck to the
          quick,   25
      Yet with my nobler reason 'gainst my fury
      Do I take part. The rarer action is
      In virtue than in vengeance. They being penitent,
      The sole drift of my purpose doth extend
      Not a frown further. Go release them, Ariel.   30
      My charms I'll break, their senses I'll restore,
      And they shall be themselves.

Ari.   I'll fetch them, sir.
                                       Exit.

Pros. Ye elves of hills, brooks, standing lakes, and
          groves,
      And ye that on the sands with printless foot
      Do chase the ebbing Neptune, and do fly him   35
      When he comes back; you demi-puppets that
      By moonshine do the green sour ringlets make,

Whereof the ewe not bites; and you whose pastime
Is to make midnight mushrooms, that rejoice
To hear the solemn curfew; by whose aid,   40
Weak masters though ye be, I have bedimm'd
The noontide sun, call'd forth the mutinous winds,
And 'twixt the green sea and the azur'd vault
Set roaring war; to the dread rattling thunder
Have I given fire, and rifted Jove's stout oak   45
With his own bolt; the strong-bas'd promontory
Have I made shake, and by the spurs pluck'd up
The pine and cedar; graves at my command
Have wak'd their sleepers, op'd, and let 'em forth
By my so potent art. But this rough magic   50
I here abjure, and, when I have requir'd
Some heavenly music, which even now I do,
To work mine end upon their senses that
This airy charm is for, I'll break my staff,
Bury it certain fathoms in the earth,   55
And deeper than did ever plummet sound
I'll drown my book.   *Solemn music.*

*Here enters Ariel before: then Alonso, with a frantic
     gesture, attended by Gonzalo; Sebastian and Antonio
     in like manner, attended by Adrian and Francisco.
     They all enter the circle which Prospero had made, and
     there stand charmed; which Prospero observing, speaks.*

A solemn air and the best comforter
To an unsettled fancy cure thy brains,

Now useless, boil'd within thy skull! There
    stand,   60
For you are spell-stopp'd.
Holy Gonzalo, honourable man,
Mine eyes, even sociable to the shew of thine,
Fall fellowly drops. The charm dissolves apace,
And as the morning steals upon the night,   65
Melting the darkness, so their rising senses
Begin to chase the ignorant fumes that mantle
Their clearer reason. O good Gonzalo,
My true preserver, and a loyal sir
To him thou follow'st! I will pay thy graces   70
Home both in word and deed. Most cruelly
Didst thou, Alonso, use me and my daughter.
Thy brother was a furtherer in the act.
Thou art pinch'd for't now, Sebastian. Flesh
    and blood,
You, brother mine, that entertain'd ambition,   75
Expell'd remorse and nature, whom, with Sebastian,
Whose inward pinches therefore are most strong,
Would here have kill'd your king, I do forgive thee,
Unnatural though thou art. Their understanding
Begins to swell, and the approaching tide   80
Will shortly fill the reasonable shore
That now lies foul and muddy. Not one of them
That yet looks on me, or would know me! Ariel,
Fetch me the hat and rapier in my cell;
I will discase me, and myself present   85

As I was sometime Milan.   Quickly, spirit ;
Thou shalt ere long be free.

Ariel sings and helps to attire him.

Ari. "Where the bee sucks, there suck I.
    In a cowslip's bell I lie ;
    There I couch when owls do cry.   **90**
    On the bat's back I do fly
    After summer merrily.
Merrily, merrily shall I live now
Under the blossom that hangs on the bough."

Pros. Why, that's my dainty Ariel ! I shall miss thee ;
    But yet thou shalt have freedom.   So, so, so.   **96**
    To the King's ship, invisible as thou art ;
    There shalt thou find the mariners asleep
    Under the hatches.   The master and the boat-
      swain
    Being awake, enforce them to this place,   **100**
    And presently, I prithee.
Ari. I drink the air before me, and return
    Or ere your pulse twice beat.   *Exit.*
Gon. All torment, trouble, wonder, and amazement
    Inhabits here.   Some heavenly power guide us   **105**
    Out of this fearful country !
Pros.   Behold, sir King,
    The wronged Duke of Milan, Prospero.
    For more assurance that a living prince

Does now speak to thee, I embrace thy body ;
And to thee and thy company I bid   110
A hearty welcome.

Alon.   Whe'er thou be'st he or no,
Or some enchanted trifle to abuse me,
As late I have been, I not know. Thy pulse
Beats as of flesh and blood ; and, since I saw thee,
The affliction of my mind amends, with which,   115
I fear, a madness held me. This must crave,
An if this be at all, a most strange story.
Thy dukedom I resign and do entreat
Thou pardon me my wrongs. But how should Prospero
Be living and be here ?

Pros.   First, noble friend,   120
Let me embrace thine age, whose honour cannot
Be measur'd or confin'd.

Gon.   Whether this be
Or be not, I'll not swear.

Pros.   You do yet taste
Some subtleties o' the isle, that will not let you
Believe things certain. Welcome, my friends all !
[*Aside to Seb. and Ant.*] But you, my brace of lords, were I so minded,   126
I here could pluck his Highness' frown upon you
And justify you traitors. At this time
I will tell no tales.

Seb.   [*Aside.*] The devil speaks in him.

Pros. No.

For you, most wicked sir, whom to call brother 130
Would even infect my mouth, I do forgive
Thy rankest fault ; all of them ; and require
My dukedom of thee, which perforce, I know,
Thou must restore.

Alon. If thou be'st Prospero,
Give us particulars of thy preservation, 135
How thou hast met us here, whom three hours since
Were wreck'd upon this shore, where I have lost —
How sharp the point of this remembrance is ! —
My dear son Ferdinand.

Pros. I am woe for't, sir.

Alon. Irreparable is the loss, and Patience 140
Says it is past her cure.

Pros. I rather think
You have not sought her help, of whose soft grace
For the like loss I have her sovereign aid
And rest myself content.

Alon. You the like loss !

Pros. As great to me as late ; and, supportable 145
To make the dear loss, have I means much weaker
Than you may call to comfort you, for I
Have lost my daughter.

Alon. A daughter ?
O heavens, that they were living both in Naples,
The King and Queen there ! That they were, I
wish 150

Myself were mudded in that oozy bed
Where my son lies. When did you lose your
    daughter ?

Pros. In this last tempest. I perceive, these lords
At this encounter do so much admire
That they devour their reason and scarce think
Their eyes do offices of truth, their words   156
Are natural breath ; but, howsoe'er you have
Been justled from your senses, know for certain
That I am Prospero and that very duke
Which was thrust forth of Milan, who most
    strangely   160
Upon this shore, where you were wreck'd, was
    landed,
To be the lord on't. No more yet of this ;
For 'tis a chronicle of day by day,
Not a relation for a breakfast nor
Befitting this first meeting. Welcome, sir ;   165
This cell's my court. Here have I few attendants,
And subjects none abroad. Pray you, look in
My dukedom since you have given me again,
I will requite you with as good a thing ;
At least bring forth a wonder, to content ye   170
As much as me my dukedom.

Here Prospero discovers Ferdinand and Miranda playing
at chess.

Mir. Sweet lord, you play me false.

Fer.   No, my dearest love,
  I would not for the world.

Mir. Yes, for a score of kingdoms you should wrangle,
  And I would call it fair play.

Alon.   If this prove   175
  A vision of the island, one dear son
  Shall I twice lose.

Seb.   A most high miracle !

Fer. Though the seas threaten, they are merciful ;
  I have curs'd them without cause.   [*Kneels.*]

Alon.   Now all the blessings
  Of a glad father compass thee about !   180
  Arise, and say how thou cam'st here.

Mir.   O, wonder !
  How many goodly creatures are there here !
  How beauteous mankind is !   O brave new world,
  That has such people in't !

Pros.   'Tis new to thee.

Alon. What is this maid with whom thou wast at play ?
  Your eld'st acquaintance cannot be three hours. 186
  Is she the goddess that hath sever'd us,
  And brought us thus together ?

Fer.   Sir, she is mortal,
  But by immortal Providence she's mine.
  I chose her when I could not ask my father   190
  For his advice, nor thought I had one.   She
  Is daughter to this famous Duke of Milan,
  Of whom so often I have heard renown,

But never saw before ; of whom I have
Receiv'd a second life ; and second father   195
This lady makes him to me.

Alon.   I am hers.
But, O, how oddly will it sound that I
Must ask my child forgiveness !

Pros.   There, sir, stop.
Let us not burden our remembrances with
A heaviness that's gone.

Gon.   I have inly wept,   200
Or should have spoke ere this. Look down, you gods,
And on this couple drop a blessed crown !
For it is you that have chalk'd forth the way
Which brought us hither.

Alon.   I say, Amen, Gonzalo !

Gon. Was Milan thrust from Milan, that his issue   205
Should become Kings of Naples ? O, rejoice
Beyond a common joy, and set it down
With gold on lasting pillars : in one voyage
Did Claribel her husband find at Tunis,
And Ferdinand, her brother, found a wife   210
Where he himself was lost, Prospero his dukedom
In a poor isle, and all of us ourselves
When no man was his own.

Alon.   [*To Fer. and Mir.*] Give me your hands.
Let grief and sorrow still embrace his heart
That doth not wish you joy !

Gon.   Be it so ! Amen !

Re-enter Ariel, with the Master and Boatswain amazedly
following.

O, look, sir, look, sir! here is more of us.   216
I prophesi'd, if a gallows were on land,
This fellow could not drown.   Now, blasphemy,
That swear'st grace o'erboard, not an oath on
          shore?
Hast thou no mouth by land?   What is the
          news?

Boats.   The best news is, that we have safely found   221
Our king and company; the next, our ship —
Which, but three glasses since, we gave out split —
Is tight and yare and bravely rigg'd as when
We first put out to sea.

Ari.   [*Aside to Pros.*] Sir, all this service   225
Have I done since I went.

Pros.   [*Aside to Ari.*] My tricksy spirit!

Alon. These are not natural events; they strengthen
From strange to stranger.   Say, how came you
          hither?

Boats. If I did think, sir, I were well awake,
I'd strive to tell you.   We were dead of sleep,   230
And — how we know not — all clapp'd under
          hatches;
Where but even now with strange and several
          noises
Of roaring, shrieking, howling, jingling chains,

And moe diversity of sounds, all horrible,
We were awak'd; straightway, at liberty;   235
Where we, in all her trim, freshly beheld
Our royal, good, and gallant ship, our master
Cap'ring to eye her. On a trice, so please you,
Even in a dream, were we divided from them
And were brought moping hither.

Ari.   [*Aside to Pros.*] Was't well done?

Pros. [*Aside to Ari.*] Bravely, my diligence. Thou
        shalt be free.   241

Alon. This is as strange a maze as e'er men trod;
And there is in this business more than nature
Was ever conduct of. Some oracle
Must rectify our knowledge.

Pros.   Sir, my liege,   245
Do not infest your mind with beating on
The strangeness of this business. At pick'd
        leisure,
Which shall be shortly, single I'll resolve you,
Which to you shall seem probable, of every
These happen'd accidents; till when, be cheerful
And think of each thing well. [*Aside to Ari.*] Come
        hither, spirit.   251
Set Caliban and his companions free;
Untie the spell. [*Exit Ariel.*] How fares my gra-
        cious sir?
There are yet missing of your company
Some few odd lads that you remember not.   255

H

*Re-enter Ariel, driving in Caliban, Stephano, and Trin-
culo, in their stolen apparel.*

Ste. Every man shift for all the rest, and let no
    man take care for himself ; for all is but for-
    tune.   Coragio, bully-monster, coragio !

Trin. If these be true spies which I wear in my
    head, here's a goodly sight.   260

Cal. O Setebos, these be brave spirits indeed !
    How fine my master is !   I am afraid
    He will chastise me.

Seb.   Ha, ha !
    What things are these, my lord Antonio ?
    Will money buy 'em ?

Ant.   Very like ; one of them
    Is a plain fish, and, no doubt, marketable.   266

Pros. Mark but the badges of these men, my lords,
    Then say if they be true.   This mis-shapen knave,
    His mother was a witch, and one so strong
    That could control the moon, make flows and
        ebbs,
    And deal in her command without her power.   271
    These three have robb'd me ; and this demi-
        devil —
    For he's a bastard one — had plotted with them
    To take my life.   Two of these fellows you
    Must know and own ; this thing of darkness I   275
    Acknowledge mine.

Cal.   I shall be pinch'd to death.

Alon. Is not this Stephano, my drunken butler?

Seb. He is drunk now.   Where had he wine?

Alon. And Trinculo is reeling ripe.   Where should they

    Find this grand liquor that hath gilded 'em?   280
    How cam'st thou in this pickle?

Trin. I have been in such a pickle since I saw you
    last that, I fear me, will never out of my bones.
    I shall not fear fly-blowing.

Seb. Why, how now, Stephano!   285

Ste. O, touch me not; I am not Stephano, but a
    cramp.

Pros. You'd be king o' the isle, sirrah?

Ste. I should have been a sore one then.

Alon. This is a strange thing as e'er I look'd on.

                      Pointing to Caliban.

Pros. He is as disproportion'd in his manners   290
    As in his shape.   Go, sirrah, to my cell;
    Take with you your companions.   As you look
    To have my pardon, trim it handsomely.

Cal. Ay, that I will; and I'll be wise hereafter
    And seek for grace.   What a thrice-doubled ass   295
    Was I, to take this drunkard for a god
    And worship this dull fool!

Pros.   Go to; away!

Alon. Hence, and bestow your luggage where you
    found it.

Seb. Or stole it, rather.

[*Exeunt Cal., Ste., and Trin.*]

Pros. Sir, I invite your Highness and your train   300
    To my poor cell, where you shall take your rest
    For this one night; which, part of it, I'll waste
    With such discourse as, I not doubt, shall make it
    Go quick away, — the story of my life
    And the particular accidents gone by   305
    Since I came to this isle.   And in the morn
    I'll bring you to your ship and so to Naples,
    Where I have hope to see the nuptial
    Of these our dear-belov'd solemnized;
    And thence retire me to my Milan, where   310
    Every third thought shall be my grave.

Alon.   I long
    To hear the story of your life, which must
    Take the ear strangely.

Pros.   I'll deliver all;
    And promise you calm seas, auspicious gales,
    And sail so expeditious that shall catch   315
    Your royal fleet far off. [*Aside to Ari.*] My
       Ariel, chick,
    That is thy charge.   Then to the elements
    Be free, and fare thou well! Please you, draw
       near.   *Exeunt omnes.*

EPILOGUE

Now my charms are all o'erthrown,
And what strength I have's mine own,
Which is most faint.   Now, 'tis true,
I must be here confin'd by you,
Or sent to Naples.   Let me not,   5
Since I have my dukedom got
And pardon'd the deceiver, dwell
In this bare island by your spell;
But release me from my bands
With the help of your good hands.   10
Gentle breath of yours my sails
Must fill, or else my project fails,
Which was to please.   Now I want
Spirits to enforce, art to enchant,
And my ending is despair,   15
Unless I be reliev'd by prayer,
Which pierces so that it assaults
Mercy itself and frees all faults.
As you from crimes would pardon'd be,
Let your indulgence set me free.   *Exit.*   20

Notes

A list of the " Names of the Actors " was given in the First Folio at the end of the play. The notes of place, and the stage directions that are inclosed in brackets, were added by eighteenth century editors.

I. i. 9. if room enough. Sea room. The ship is near a lee shore in a gale of wind; she is seaworthy, and the boatswain cares not how much wind there may be, if the ship has room enough to work in.

I. i. 15. assist the storm. By getting in our way.

I. i. 17. cares. Singular verbs with plural subjects are common in Shakespeare. Perhaps the *-s* is here a survival of the Northern plural, as in IV. i. 264 and V. i. 105. It may be due to carelessness; see I. ii. 478, and V. i. 216.

I. i. 18. these roarers. The winds and waves. Perhaps an allusion to the Elizabethan use of " roarer " to mean a blustering bully.

I. i. 31. no drowning mark . . . perfect gallows. A reference to the proverb, " He that's born to be hanged need fear no drowning." See lines 35, 49, and 61, and V. i. 217.

I. i. 34. rope of his destiny. The hangman's rope.

I. i. 39. louder than . . . our office. " Prayers might well be in the heart and lips, but drowned in the outcries of the officers." — Strachey's *Reportory.* See Introduction.

I. i. 49. for. *I.e.,* against.

I. i. 52. lay her a-hold. Keep her close to the wind.

I. i. 56. must our mouths be cold? In death.

I. i. 61. **the washing of ten tides.** " Pirates and robbers by sea are condemned in the court of admiraltie, and hanged on the shore at low water marke, where they are left till three tides have overwashed them." — Harrison's *Description of England* (1577). Three tides are not enough for this scoundrel.

I. i. 70, 71. **long heath, brown furze.** *Long heath* is the name of a distinct plant. Notwithstanding this, Hanmer's emendation has been adopted by many editors; " ling. heath, broom, furze."

I. ii. 2-5. The storm " swelling and roaring . . . at length did beate all light from heaven; which like a hell of darkness turned blacke upon us . . . the sea swelled above the clouds, and gave battle unto heaven." — Strachey's *Reportory.*

I. ii. 5. **fire.** Two syllables.

I. ii. 7. **creature.** Perhaps a collective noun; creatures.

I. ii. 10. **god of power.** Powerful god. Cf. line 55.

I. ii. 11. **or ere.** Before. In this redundant locution *or* and *ere* are both derived from Anglo-Saxon *ær,* and each means " before."

I. ii. 14. **your.** Miranda in this scene addresses her father with the respectful " you"; except in this line, Prospero addresses his daughter with the affectionate and familiar " thou."

I. ii. 19. **more better.** Double comparatives and superlatives are frequent in Shakespeare. Cf. " more braver," I. ii. 439, and " worser," IV. i. 27.

I. ii. 21, 22. **more to know . . . thoughts.** The thought of knowing more never entered into my mind.

I. ii. 29. **No soul —** Lost, Prospero was about to add.

I. ii. 43. Tell me the image of anything that.

I. ii. 53. A nine-syllable line, beginning with an accented word.

I. ii. 66. **My brother.** The predicate for this nominative, — if, indeed, there is one, — is "created," line 81. This play contains many instances of anacoluthon, of broken sentences such as frequently occur in actual conversation, especially under the stress of emotion.

I. ii. 80. **who.** Shakespeare frequently neglects to use the inflected form "whom." Cf. I. ii. 231; IV. i. 4.

I. ii. 81. **To trash for overtopping.** To hold in check, as hounds which outran the pack were held back by a weight fastened about the neck. *Overtopping*, however, seems a term from gardening rather than from hunting.

I. ii. 87. **Thou attendst not.** These and other similar remarks and questions serve to break up Prospero's long narrative, and to give an air of reality to the conversation.

I. ii. 94. **Like a good parent.** "A father above the common rate of men has commonly a son below it." — Johnson.

I. ii. 98. **revenue.** The second syllable is accented.

I. ii. 99–102. **like one . . . his own lie.** Like one who having by telling a lie made his memory such a sinner unto truth that it credited his own lie. In l. 100, *into* means unto, and *it* refers to *lie*, l. 102.

I. ii. 104. **executing the outer face of royalty.** Performing the external duties of royalty; keeping up the appearances.

I. ii. 107. **To have no screen.** To remove Prospero, who stood between the substitute and complete sovereignty ("absolute Milan").

I. ii. 109. **Me.** For me.

I. ii. 123. **in lieu o'.** In return for; not " in place of."

I. ii. 144. **aboard a bark.** Milan appears to be a seaport in this play, — as also in *The Two Gentlemen of Verona.*

I. ii. 146. **a butt.** The meaning of this word is not certainly known. The emendation " boat," by Rowe (1709), is not to be accepted. Italian *botto*, a sloop-rigged galliot with flattish bottom, has been suggested by Brinsley Nicholson. *Butt* may perhaps be an imitation of *botto* in a lost Italian story upon which *The Tempest* is based.

I. ii. 152. **a cherubin.** The Chaldee plural of cherub, used as a singular. This has become the standard form in French, Spanish, and Italian, but not in English.

I. ii. 173. **than other princess can.** Than other princesses are able to profit.

I. ii. 181–184. The crisis in Prospero's life, because his star is now at the zenith. The same thought is expressed by a different metaphor in the familiar lines, *Julius Cæsar*, IV. iii. 218–221. Note the word " omit " in both passages.

I. ii. 186. **give it way.** Yield to it.

I. ii. 187. **away.** Hither.

I. ii. 189. The name Ariel (variously interpreted, perhaps meaning " altar of God ") occurs several times in *Isaiah* xxix. The meaning that Shakespeare intended, — " an ayrie spirit," — is indicated in the list of characters.

I. ii. 196–210. Strachey's *Reportory* has a description of the phenomenon known as St. Elmo's fire. The word " amazement " occurs three times.

I. ii. 229. **Bermoothes.** An attempt to indicate the Spanish pronunciation of Bermudez, the name of the discoverer of the Bermuda Islands. The word "from " makes it clear that Prospero's island was not one of the Bermudas, though the accounts of those islands supplied material for the play.

I. ii. 230. **under hatches stow'd.** Cf. V. i. 99, 231. "Being utterly spent were even resolved without any hope of their lives to shut up the hatches." — Jourdan's *Discovery*.

I. ii. 232. **asleep.** "They were so overwearied . . . and spent with long . . . continuance of their labour that for the most part they were fallen asleep in corners." — Jourdan's *Discovery*.

I. ii. 240. **two glasses.** Two hours. See note on V. i. 223.

I. ii. 258. **Sycorax.** The meaning of this name is uncertain. Various suggestions have been made, *e.g.*, the Greek words for sow (σῦς) and raven (κόραξ), both of them associated with witchcraft. Cf. *Macbeth*, I. iii. 2, and I. v. 39.

I. ii. 266. **for one thing she did.** Not indicated in the play; perhaps mentioned in the lost story or play on which *The Tempest* is based. Charles Lamb refers to an account by John Ogilby of a witch who saved Algier from an attack by Charles V. Yet another suggestion is that Shakespeare never troubled himself to decide what the "one thing" might be.

I. ii. 284. **Caliban.** Usually explained as a metathesis of Canibal, for Caribal, a Carib, native of the Caribbee Islands. Though the Caribs are said to have been cannibals, it is not intended to imply that Caliban was an eater of human flesh. Another suggestion is that the name comes from the region called Calibia, and that "Shake-

speare possibly inherited the name from the old story or
drama which is the foundation of the play." Caliban,
says Mr. Luce, plays the part of " an Indian, a hag-born
monstrosity, and a (negro) slave."

I. ii. 326. **urchins.** Originally hedgehogs; then the
goblins that took the form of hedgehogs. Cf. II. ii. 5.

I. ii. 329. **as thick as** (the cells in) **honeycomb.**

I. ii. 334. **water with berries in't.** " The islands are
full of Shawes of goodly Cedar . . . the berries whereof,
our men seething, straining, and letting stand some three
or foure daies, made a kind of pleasant drinke." — Strachey's
Reportory.

I. ii. 338. **The fresh springs, brine-pits.** " Sure it is,
that there are no Rivers nor running Springs of fresh
water to be found on any of them; when we came first
we digged and found certaine gushings and soft bublings."
— Strachey's *Reportory.* Jourdan states that the crew
were compelled to make salt there.

I. ii. 342, 352. **which.** Shakespeare frequently uses
which for who or whom, as in III. i. 6 and V. i. 160. Cf.
"Our Father, which art."

I. ii. 351. In the Folios this speech is assigned to Miranda. It was transferred to Prospero on the ground that
it is more appropriate for him, and that it was he, not
Miranda, who had taught Caliban.

I. ii. 364. **The red plague.** So named because of the
color of the sore, which was sometimes red, sometimes
yellow, sometimes black. Sometimes explained as leprosy;
and as erysipelas. Cf. *Coriolanus*, IV. i. 13.

I. ii. 370. **aches.** Pronounced aitches. Cf. *Much Ado*,
III. iv. 54–56.

I. ii. 373. **Setebos.** Shakespeare probably found this name in Eden's *History of Travaile* (1577), where mention is made of the "great devil," or chief god, of the Patagonians. In the same work Shakespeare may have found the names Alonso, Sebastian, Antonio, Ferdinand, and Gonzales.

I. ii. 378, 379. **kiss'd The wild waves whist.** Kissed the wild waves into silence; or, as Allen suggested, by kissing one another brought the waves to hushed attention. In some of the old dances it was customary to kiss partners at the beginning: see *Henry VIII*, I. iv. 95. From lines 391–393 we learn that it was Ariel's music that quieted the waves. This favors the interpretation of "the wild waves whist" as an absolute construction, therefore to be followed by a comma.

I. ii. 381. *Burden.* Refrain; or a deep, droning bass, frequently sung throughout the stanza. Here the "sweet sprites" and "the watch-dogs" bear the burden to Ariel's singing.

I. ii. 390. **again.** Again and again.

I. ii. 408. **The fringed . . . advance.** Raise your eyelids. Cf. *Pericles*, III. iii. 99–103.

I. ii. 421. **Most sure, the goddess.** Cf. V. i. 187; also, *O dea certe, Æneid*, I. 328.

I. ii. 422. **these airs.** Played and sung by Ariel.

I. ii. 438. **his brave son.** Not mentioned again. To be explained either as a character at first planned for and afterward forgotten or omitted; or as a character that appeared in the lost original of *The Tempest*. Fleay suggested that "Francisco (II. i. 113) is what is left of him."

I. ii. 439. **more braver.** See note on I. ii. 19.

I. ii. 441. **They have changed eyes.** Exchanged looks of love.

I. ii. 443. **Have done yourself some wrong.** Have misrepresented yourself.

I. ii. 468. **not fearful.** Not terrible or dangerous.

I. ii. 469. **My foot my tutor?** My inferior my instructor?

II. i. The cheap and tiresome wit of this scene is indicative of the slender mental equipment and of the cynical indifference of the conspirators. Only the good and garrulous Gonzalo expresses gratitude for preservation, or speaks words of good cheer to his companions.

II. i. 11. **visitor.** One who brings spiritual consolation to the sick; note line 10.

II. i. 13. **the watch . . . will strike.** Early watches, "Nuremberg eggs," were in reality small clocks that struck the hours. They were too large for the pocket.

II. i. 36. **Ha, ha, ha?** The Folios divide this line between Sebastian and Antonio. Theobald and later editors give the entire line to Sebastian, who, immediately upon losing, — when Adrian begins to crow, — pays his bet by laughing.

II. i. 42, 46, 49. " Yet did we find there the ayre so temperate and the country so abundantly fruitfull of all fit necessaries for the sustentation and preservation of man's life." — Jourdan's *Discovery*.

II. i. 82–85. Tunis is a few miles from the site of ancient Carthage, of which Dido is reputed to have been queen.

II. i. 86. **more than the miraculous harp.** More powerful than the harp of Amphion, which raised the walls of Thebes; or of Apollo, which raised the walls of Troy.

II. i. 120. **his.** See note on II. i. 163.

II. i. 127. **Who.** The antecedent may be " she," or
" eye ; " or, perhaps, the you implied in *your* — the eye
of you who.

II. i. 131. **Which end . . . should bow.** The subject
of the verb, — either she or it, — is omitted.

II. i. 148–164. Gonzalo's description of an imaginary
commonwealth follows closely the translation (1603)
by John Florio of Montaigne's Essay, " Of the Caniballes."

II. i. 163. **it own kind.** The early form of *it* was "hit,"
possessive " his." " Its " was not used by Spenser,
did not occur in the original edition of the King James
Bible (see *Genesis* iii. 5), and occurs only three times in
the poems of Milton. " It " possessive occurs fourteen
times in the plays of Shakespeare. " Its " occurs ten
times, — in this play in I. ii. 95 and 395. Instances of
the avoidance of the word occur in I. ii. 295 and II. i. 120.

II. i. 183. **lift the moon out of her sphere.** According
to the Ptolemaic system, the moon, sun, and planets were
each set in a sphere revolving about the earth at the center.

II. i. 185. **and then go a bat-fowling.** Because nights
when there was no moon were best for bat-fowling: see
Glossary. " Which birds with a light bough in a darke
night (as in our Lowbelling) wee caught." — Strachey's
Reportory.

II. i. 187. **adventure my discretion.** Risk my reputation for discretion.

II. i. 220. **if** (you) **heed me.**

II. i. 221. **Trebles thee o'er.** Makes you three times
as great. **I am standing water.** I am quiet, between ebb
and flow, ready to listen.

II. i. 223–228. O, if you knew how you encourage my design by yon mocking metaphor; how in striving to turn it to naught, you give it more meaning! Hesitating, retreating, men are often near to running aground because of their fear or sloth.

II i. 232–234. **Although this lord . . . is earth'd.** Although this lord (Gonzalo) of failing memory, who, when he is buried, shall be as little remembered as he now remembers.

II. i. 238. **As.** As that.

II. i. 243. **But doubt discovery.** Without doubting the power of discernment.

II. i. 247. **beyond man's life.** Farther than one can travel in a man's lifetime.

II. i. 250. **from whom.** Coming from whom.

II. i. 251. **some cast again.** Some cast ashore. Also, in the language of the stage, *cast* for new parts. This use appears to have suggested the stage terms *act, prologue*, and *discharge*, in the following lines.

II. i. 259. **us.** The cubits. — **Keep.** Let her keep.

II. i. 265, 266. **make A chough of as deep chat.** Cause a jackdaw to chatter as wisely; or become a chatterer equally profound.

II. i. 278. **consciences.** Probably to be pronounced as two syllables, not sounding the final *s*. Cf. V. i. 199.

II. i. 283. This line is an Alexandrine.

II. i. 284. **doing thus.** With a stab, — indicated by a motion.

II. i. 289. **They'll tell the clock . . . hour.** Count the strokes, follow any hint or example that we give.

II. i. 296. **fall.** Transitive, as often. Cf. V. i. 64.

II. i. 326, 327. Apparently the only intentional riming couplet in the play, — except the songs and the Masque in Act IV.

II. ii. 6. **like a firebrand.** Such as the Will-o'-the-Wisp.

II. ii. 28–30. **in England . . . a piece of silver.** Malone quotes a license granted by Sir H. Herbert, Master of the Revels, " To shew a strange fish for half a yeare, the 3rd of September, 1632."

II. ii. 29. **this fish painted.** On a board outside a booth at a fair.

II. ii. 31, 32. **make a man.** A play upon words, with the secondary meaning " make a man's fortune."

II. ii. 34. **a dead Indian.** Perhaps an allusion to the Indians brought home by Martin Frobisher on more than one of his voyages. Others were brought to England in the years shortly preceding the writing of this play.

II. ii. 35. **Legg'd like a man! and his fins like arms!** Mr. Luce cites the "following first sketch (*circa* 1597; Purchas, II. 1556) of the sole inhabitant of the Bermudas : — ' A sea-monster . . . armes like a man without haire, and at the elbows great Finnes like a fish.' "

II. ii. 63. **on four legs.** On crutches.

II. ii. 80. **I will not take too much for him.** *I.e.*, no sum can be too much.

II. ii. 83. **trembling.** A sign of possession by the evil one.

II. ii. 86. **give language to you, cat.** An allusion to the proverb, " Good liquor will make a cat speak."

II. ii. 98. **Amen!** Enough, make an end.

II. ii. 103. **no long spoon.** Referring to the familiar

I

proverb, " He must have a long spoon that must eat with the devil." *Comedy of Errors*, IV. iii. 62.

II. ii. 121. **celestial liquor.** Cf. the *divine liqueur* and the *vin divin* of Rabelais, V. 45, 46.

II. ii. 134. **kiss the book.** The bottle, if you are going to take an oath.

II. ii. 142, 144. **the man i' the moon . . . dog and thy bush.** Said in olden time to be the man who broke the Sabbath by gathering sticks (*Numbers* xv. 32). Cf. *A Midsummer-Night's Dream*, V. i. 136.

II. ii. 142. **when time was.** Once upon a time.

II. ii. 172. **long nails . . . dig thee pignuts.** Earth-nuts, which are rooted up and eaten by pigs.

II. ii. 176. **Young scamels from the rock.** The most debated passage in the play. Scamel is a name applied to the bar-tailed godwit, regarded as a delicacy; see article " Godwit," eleventh edition of the *Encyc. Brit.* This bird, however, breeds in the fens, not in the rocks. There is little reason for supposing that the word means a limpet or shell-fish, as some editors have asserted. If any change in the text is needed, the slightest and the most probable is that of *c* to *e*; this gives sea-mell, sea-mall, a sea-mew or sea-gull, esteemed a delicacy. " Another sea-fowle there is, that lyeth in little holes in the ground, like unto a coney-hole, and are in great numbers exceeding good meat, very fat and sweet." — Jourdan's *Discovery.* In Strachey's *Reportory* this fowl is described as the "Sea Owle," and compared to a " sea-meawe."

III. i. 2. **sets off.** The subject of this verb, also the object, may be either " labour " or " delight." (1) The toil sets off, or heightens by contrast, the delight. (2)

The delight offsets, counterbalances, is a set-off against the toil. The latter interpretation is more in harmony with lines 6, 7, and 13, 14.

III. i. 3, 4. **most poor . . . rich ends.** The humblest undertakings have in view rich rewards.

III. i. 13. **like executor.** A similar performer.

III. i. 15. **Most busy least, when I do it.** The most difficult passage in this play, — perhaps in all of the plays; it has probably called forth more comment than any other passage by Shakespeare. Of the numerous editors and commentators cited by Furness in his twelve octavo pages of notes, practically all agree that the passage means that Ferdinand is most busy when he is thinking of Miranda, that is, when he appears to be least busy. "I forget," he says, "to do my work: but these sweet thoughts of her make me all the more able and willing to work, so that my moments of apparent idleness make me a more efficient worker." The First Folio reads "Most busie lest," *i.e.*, least; the other Folios read "Most busie least." Numerous emendations have been suggested; "Most busiest" is as good as any.

Do it. (1) My work; or (2) when I think of Miranda.

III. i. 16. **[at a distance, unseen].** This stage direction was added by Rowe (1709), when the character and setting of the theater had changed. In 1611 Prospero probably appeared upon the balcony overlooking the stage. He was thus visible to the audience, unseen (conventionally) by Ferdinand and Miranda. Cf. Stage direction, III. iii. 17.

III. i. 21. **He's safe.** From interfering with us.

III. i. 29, 30. An unintentional rime. See also lines 23–25, and III. iii. 49–51. Brinsley Nicholson sees in these rimes unintentional survivals of some older play that was used by Shakespeare.

III. i. 31, 32. **infected . . . visitation.** Terms that were in common use when the plague was frequent. Cf. *Love's Labour's Lost*, V. ii. 419–422.

III. i. 61. **and would no more.** And but "for your sake" (line 66), would no more.

III. i. 70, 71. **invert . . . mischief.** Change to mischief the best that is promised me.

III. i. 78. **take.** Dare take. Cf. line 77.

III. i. 80. **it.** Her unnamed love for Ferdinand.

III. i. 87. **thus humble.** He is kneeling.

III. i. 94. **my book.** Of magic; his conjuring-book. Cf. I. iii. 167; III. ii. 97, 103.

III. ii. 1. **Tell not me.** Don't talk to me.

III. ii. 22. **go.** Walk. **lie.** A pun; so, also, *standard* (line 20).

III. ii. 52. **jesting monkey.** Because Trinculo, who was supposed to have spoken, was the king's jester.

III. ii. 92. **Stand farther off.** Perhaps because of the " very ancient and fish-like smell."

III. ii. 104. **utensils.** To be accented on the first syllable.

III. ii. 108. **nonpareil.** So in the *True Relation*, etc. . . . *Newes from Virginia* (1608), Pocahontas, the daughter of Powhatan, is described as " the only *Nonpareil* of his Country."

III. ii. 136. **the picture of Nobody.** Perhaps suggested by a print that appeared on the title page of *Nobody and*

Somebody, a comedy published in 1606. The figure had head, arms, and legs, but no body.

III. ii. 143–152. "You shall heare in the ayre the sound of tabers and other instruments, to put the travellers in feare, &c., by evill spirits that make these soundes and also do call . . . travellers by their names." Chap. 36 of the *Book* of Marco Polo, translated by John Frampton, 1579.

III. iii. 11. **he's so out of hope.** It is hopeless to make longer search for him.

III. iii. 17, stage direction. ***Prospero on the top invisible.*** On the balcony at the back of the stage. See note on III. i. 16.

III. iii. 21. **a living drollery.** A puppet-show in which the characters are alive, not wooden dolls.

III. iii. 23. **one tree . . . one phœnix.** "As there is but one *Phœnix* in the world, so is there but one tree in Arabia, wherein she buildeth." John Lyly's *Euphues and his England* (1580). Cf. Shakespeare's *The Phœnix and the Turtle*, and also Pliny's *Natural History*, Book X.

III. iii. 39. **Praise in departing.** A proverbial expression. Do not praise your entertainment too soon; wait till you see how it will end.

III. iii. 44–46. **Who would believe . . . wallets of flesh?** Commonly supposed to refer to the goitre, which is not, however, so rare a disease, even in England, as to appear incredible. Furness cites from a compilation of travelers' tales in the Middle Ages a mention of Satyrs who "cary their meat under their chin as in a store-house, and from thence being hungry they take it forth to eate." He suggested that "the Pouched Apes gave rise to the story."

III. iii. 47. **men Whose heads stood in their breasts.**
Cf. *Othello*, I. iii. 144: " men whose heads Do grow beneath
their shoulders." Reports of this kind might have been
seen by Shakespeare in the *Travels* of Sir John Mande-
ville, in Sir Walter Raleigh's *Discovery of Guiana* (1596),
and in Hakluyt's *Voyages* (1598).

III. iii. 48. **each putter out of five for one.** Each
traveler who insures at the rate of five for one. Cf. Ben
Jonson's *Every Man out of his Humour*, II. i: " I do intend
. . . to travel: and . . . I am determined to put forth
some five thousand pound, to be paid me, five for one,
upon the return of myself, my wife, and my dog from the
Turk's court in Constantinople. If all, or either of us
miscarry in the journey, 'tis gone : if we be successful, why,
there will be five and twenty thousand pound to entertain
time withal."

III. iii. 52. **stage direction.** *like a harpy.* A reminis-
cence of the harpies in Virgil's *Æneid*, III. 211–257.

III. iii. 62. **whom.** Which. Cf. III. ii. 342, 352; III. i. 6.

III. iii. 77. **worse than any death Can be at once.**
Worse than any sudden or instantaneous death can be.

III. iii. 86. **with good life.** In a lifelike manner.

III. iii. 87. **observation strange.** Unusually observant
care.

III. iii. 106. **to bite.** To eat into, to cause anguish to.

IV. i. 3. **a third of mine own life.** Variously explained,
as (1) one third of that for which he has lived, — self,
wife, and daughter (or self, daughter, and dukedom), or
(2) by metathesis from thrid, or thread, a fibre of my own
life.

IV. i. 26. **opportune.** The second syllable is accented.

IV. i. 27. **our worser genius.** Bad angel, or attendant spirit. Cf. I. ii. 457, 458. For the double comparative " worser " (used sixteen times by Shakespeare), compare " more better," I. ii. 19, and " more braver," I. ii. 439.

IV. i. 54. **good night.** Farewell to.

IV. i. 56. **my liver.** Supposed to be the seat of passion.

IV. i. 59. **No tongue!** . . . **Be silent.** Since otherwise the spell would be marred.

IV. i. 60–117; 128–138. The Masque is in couplets, to set it off from the rest of the scene. Brief as it is, it has the characteristic features of the Court Masque, — mythological characters presented in allegorical action, with the help of music, song, and dance, and introducing the " masque proper " or graceful dance (ll. 132–138). The various performances of the " divers Spirits " l. 255, and of the " strange shapes," III. iii. stage directions, ll. 17 and 83, may be compared with the " Antimasques," or grotesque dances which were also a usual feature of the Court Masques.

IV. i. 64. **pioned and twilled brims.** A much-debated line: (1) dug or trenched, and with ridges (as in twilled cloth) thrown up along the banks; or (2) with peonies and reeds or flags along the banks. Inasmuch as certainty is impossible, the reader may choose between the prosaic and the picturesque interpretation. It will be noted that there is no mention of streams; also that the banks are to be made ready to be trimmed by spongy April.

IV. i. 66. **brown groves.** Hanmer's emendation for " broom groves," the Folio reading, which is meaningless. The broom (*Planta genista*) could not afford a shadow for the " lass-lorn bachelor."

IV. i. 89. **that . . . got.** By which Pluto gained Proserpine. See Ovid, *Metam.*, V. 363 ff.

IV. i. 93. **Paphos.** In the island of Cyprus. Venus is frequently called the "Cyprian," or "the Paphian goddess."

IV. i. 97. **Hymen's torch.** Carried in the marriage procession. Cf. line 23.

IV. i. 110. The second Folio reads "and foison," which helps the meter.

IV. i. 114. **Spring . . . harvest.** The best interpretation of this couplet is Mrs. Kemble's: — "that spring shall rapidly succeed autumn, leaving the dreary winter out of the calendar." She cites *Leviticus* xxvi, 5. Staunton cites *Amos* ix, 13.

IV. i. 148–158. This noble passage finds a striking parallel in Act IV. sc. iii, of *The Tragedy of Darius* (1603?) by William Alexander, afterwards Earl of Stirling.

"Let greatnesse of her glascie scepters vaunt;
 Not sceptours, no, but reeds, soone brus'd soone broken:
 And let this worldlie pomp our wits inchant.
 All fades, and scarcelie leaves behinde a token.
Those golden Pallaces, those gorgeous halles,
 With fourniture superfluouslie faire:
Those statelie courts, those sky-encountring walles
 Evanish all like vapours in the aire."

IV. i. 156. **a rack.** Thin, drifting cloud; perhaps with reference to the gauze veils behind which the characters in the masque appeared and disappeared.

IV. i. 193. **on this line.** Line, or linden tree: cf. V. i. 10, and note "Mistress line" (235). Perhaps also the *line* on which were hung the curtains just used for the masque and now used as a clothes-line.

IV. i. 222. **King Stephano!**] O peer! An allusion to the old song quoted in *Othello*, II. iii. 93.

IV. i. 231. **let's alone.** Let us go alone, — leaving Trinculo with his "frippery." Many editors have adopted Theobald's emendation, "Let's along."

IV. i. 237. **lose your hair . . . a bald jerkin.** Weak puns, — in character, — are plentiful. In Shakespeare's time clothes-lines were commonly made of hair. Some editors see here and in l. 236 an allusion to the equator.

IV. i. 239. **by line and level.** According to rule, systematically.

IV. i. 244. **pass of pate.** Stroke of wit.

IV. i. 246. **lime.** Bird-lime, — to which everything will stick. Perhaps, also another pun on "line."

IV. i. 249. **barnacles.** "There are in the north parts of Scotland . . . certain trees, whereon doe growe certain shell-fishes, . . . which falling into the water, do become fowles, whom we call Barnakles, in the north of England Brant Geese, and in Lancashire tree Geese." — Gerarde's *Herbal* (1597). Caliban probably means geese, — not shellfish.

IV. i. 261. **aged cramps.** Cramps of age, customary to old persons; cf. I. ii. 369. This use of the verbal adjective in *ed* is common in Shakespeare, as "banished years," *Richard II*, I. iii. 210.

V. i. 2, 3. **Time . . . his carriage.** Does not bend under his burden. Everything goes prosperously.

V. i. 11. **till your release.** Till you release them.

V. i. 23, 24. **sharply Passion.** The reading of the

Third and Fourth Folios and of many later editions. The
earlier Folios have a comma after *sharply*. In that case
passion is a verb, meaning grieve, feel pain or sorrow.

V. i. 33–50. **Ye elves . . . potent art.** This speech is
based upon Golding's translation (1567) of the incanta-
tion of Medea in Ovid's *Metamorphoses*, VII. 197–214.

> "Ye Ayres and Windes: ye Elves of Hilles, of Brooks, of
> Woods alone,
>   Of standing Lakes," etc.

Lines 34–40 are based upon English folk-lore, not upon
Ovid.

V. i. 37. **green sour ringlets.**   Circles of a deeper green
and of a bitter taste, supposed to have been caused by
the fairies who dance in a round by moonlight. Actually
caused by the decaying fungi, which Shakespeare had observed.

V. i. 39. **midnight mushrooms.** That spring up quickly
in the course of a night.

V. i. 40. **rejoice . . . curfew.** Because spirits could
walk abroad only between curfew and cockcrow.

V. i. 45. **Jove's stout oak.** Sacred to Jupiter. Cf. *As
You Like It*, III. ii. 249.

V. i. 60. **boil'd.** See Glossary. The First Folio reads
"boile"; this must be interpreted, "(which), now useless,
boil."

V. i. 63. **even sociable to the show.** In full sympathy
with the appearance.

V. i. 67. **ignorant fumes.** Fumes from indigestion, etc.,
were supposed to rise to the brain and cause delusions. For
the construction, cf. next note.

V. i. 81. **reasonable shore.** The shore of reason.

V. i. 86. **sometime Milan.** Formerly Duke of Milan.

V. i. 92. **after summer.** In pursuit of summer. There is no occasion for accepting Theobald's emendation of "sunset" for "summer."

V. i. 117. **if this be at all.** If this is actual reality, — not a dream.

V. i. 118. **Thy dukedom I resign.** I release, surrender; because it had been made feudatory to him by Antonio.

V. i. 119. **my wrongs.** The wrongs that I have done to you. Cf. "their high wrongs" (25), and "till your release" (11).

V. i. 121. **thine age.** Abstract for the concrete, as in I. ii. 367, and III. i. 89.

V. i. 123, 124. **taste some subtleties.** Experience some of the illusions — "enchanted trifles" (line 112). Subtleties were devices in pastry and confectionery; note the verb "taste."

V. i. 145. **as great . . . as late.** As great as it is recent. — supportable. Words in -*able* are usually accented on the penult in Shakespeare.

V. i. 146. **means much weaker.** Alonso still has a daughter; Prospero has lost his only child.

V. i. 155. **devour their reason.** In open-mouthed astonishment.

V. i. 170. **a wonder.** A play upon Miranda's name. Cf. I. ii. 426.

V. i. 171, s. d. *discovers* by drawing a curtain. *playing at chess.* In the time of Shakespeare Naples was the center of chess-playing, — the royal game. This is the only mention of chess in all the plays.

V. i. 199. **remembrances.** Three syllables; the final
s is not sounded. Cf. II. i. 278.

V. i. 205. **Was Milan . . . from Milan.** Was the
Duke of Milan thrust forth from Milan?

V. i. 223. **three glasses since.** Three hours: Cf.
line 186 and I. ii. 240; also, *All's Well*, II. i. 169. The unity
of time is strictly observed in this play. Shakespeare
appears not to have known that the seaman's glass was
an half-hour glass. This is the only error that has been
observed in his use of nautical terms.

V. i. 236. **freshly beheld.** Beheld fresh. Cf. line 221.

V. i. 238. **to eye her.** At beholding her.

V. i. 266. **a plain fish.** A mere fish, nothing more; or
(cf. lines 221, 236) plainly a fish.

V. i. 271. **deal in her command.** Wield her authority,
influence. — **without her power.** Beyond her sphere; or
without being empowered to do so.

Epilogue. Some editors, because of the irregularity
of the verse, have denied the Shakespearean authorship
of these lines. It is to be remembered, however, that the
verse of Shakespeare's latest plays, — of *The Tempest*
in particular, — is irregular; moreover the Epilogue is
an appropriate utterance for one who was about to retire
from the life of actor and dramatist. We may even
wonder whether Shakespeare may not himself have spoken
this Epilogue.

10. **help of your good hands.** Your applause. The
noise of clapping would break the spell. Cf. IV. i. 59.

11. **Gentle breath of yours.** Your good will.

18. **Mercy itself.** All-merciful God. Cf. *Merchant of
Venice*, IV. i. 195.

Textual Variants

The text in the present edition is based upon the first Folio, and the following list records the more important variations from that version.

I. i. 64–66. Mercy . . . split !] *As part of Gonzalo's speech* F; *as the "confused noise"* Capell.
    71. furze] Rowe; firrs F.
  ii. 58, 59. heir And princess] F; heir A princess Pope.
    141. set] Wright *conj.;* nor set F.
    173. princess] F; princess' S. Walker *conj.;* princes Rowe; princesses Clark and Glover.
    201. lightnings] Theobald; Lightning F.
    351. [*Pros.*] Theobald; *Mira.* F.

II. i. 36. Antonio] *Ant.* (*as speech tag*) F.
  ii. 187. trenchering] F; trencher Pope.

III. i. 15. least] F₂; lest F₁.

IV. i. 13. gift] Rowe; guest F.
    17. rite] Rowe; right F.
    110. [*Cer.*] Theobald; F *omits.*
    123. wise] F; *some copies of F are said to read* wife.
    128. winding] Rowe; windring F.

Glossary

abuse, deceive, impose upon; V. i. 112.

accidents, events, incidents; V. i. 250, 305.

admire, wonder, marvel; V. i. 154.

admired, admirable, to be wondered at; III. i. 37. Cf. I. ii. 426.

advance, lift, raise; I. ii. 408: raised, IV. i. 177.

advantage, opportunity; III. iii. 13.

affections, feelings, emotions; V. i. 18: inclinations, wishes; I. ii. 481.

ahold, "lay her ahold," keep her close to the wind; I. i. 52.

amain, with strength, power, *i.e.,* swiftly; IV. i. 74.

amazement, astonishment, anguish, terror; I. ii. 14, 198; V. i. 104.

an, a weakened form of *and* (so spelled in the Folio), meaning if; **an if** (*and if*) is really if if; II. i. 181; II. ii. 120; IV. i. 239; V. i. 117. Cf. *Matthew* xxiv. 48; *Luke* xii. 45.

angle, nook, corner: "odd angle," a corner that has not been noted; I. ii. 223.

anon, soon, presently; II. ii. 83, 146.

appertaining, necessary, belonging to this state of affairs; III. i. 96.

Argier, Algiers; I. ii. 261, 265.

as, as if; II. i. 121, 203, 204; IV. i. 178: according as, if; III. ii. 84; V. i. 292: when; II. i. 319.

aspersion, sprinkling, — as if with holy water; IV. i. 18.

attached, seized, III. iii. 5.

avoid, begone; IV. i. 142.

azur'd, "azur'd vault," blue, overarching sky; V. i. 43.

backward, what lies behind; I. ii. 50.

badges, devices, coats of arms, worn by servants upon their livery; V. I. 267.

barnacles, geese; see note, IV. i. 249.

bass, utter in deep tones; III. iii. 99.

bate, abate, deduct; I. ii. 250; II. i. 100; III. iii. 85.

bat-fowling, catching birds by night with lights and poles, — sometimes with nets; see note, II. i. 185.

bear off, keep off, ward off; II. ii. 18.

bear up, put up the helm, and come up into the wind, ready for attack; III. ii. 3.

beating (in or on), working at; I. ii. 176; V. i. 246: agitated; IV. i. 163. Cf. *Hamlet*, III. i. 182, and *Richard II*, V. v. 5.

Bermoothes, Bermudas; see note, I. ii. 229.

betid, betided, happened; I. ii. 31.

blue-eyed, with blue about the eyes, haggard; I. ii. 269. Cf. *As You Like It*, III. ii. 393.

boil'd, over-heated, excited; V. i. 60. Cf. *A Winter's Tale*, III. iii. 63: *A Midsummer-Night's Dream*, V. i. 4.

bombard, a huge leathern vessel for holding liquor; II. ii. 21.

bosky, wooded, covered with shrubs; IV. i. 81.

bourn, boundary; II. i. 152.

bow, bend, dip (as of a scale); II. i. 131.

brain'd, have wits; III. ii. 8.

brine-pits, springs of salt water; I. ii. 338.

brave, fine, handsome (cf. Scots "braw"); I. ii. 6, 411, 438; *et passim.*

burden, refrain; see note, I. ii. 381.

butt, a large cask of the capacity of two hogsheads; II. ii. 125: see note on I. ii. 146.

by and by, presently, immediately; II. i. 13; II. ii. 181.

by'r, by our; III. iii. 1.

can, is (are) able — to make, provide; IV. i. 27; I. ii. 173.

candied, congealed (with cold); II. i. 279.

canker, a worm that eats into a flower; I. ii. 415: corrupt, grow venomous; IV. i. 192.

capable, having capacity for, susceptible to; I. ii. 353.

carriage, burden, that which is carried; V. i. 3.

case, condition, readiness; III. ii. 29.

cast, threw off; I. ii. 75: thrown up, vomited, see note, II. i. 251. Cf. II. ii. 128.

catch, a part-song, much like a round; III. ii. 126, 135.

certes, certainly, assuredly; III. iii. 30.

chaps, jaws; II. ii. 89. Cf. *wide-chapp'd*, I. i. 60.

charmingly, magically, by the power of some charm; IV. i. 119.

chat, chatter, prating; II. i. 266.

chirurgeonly, like a skillful surgeon; II. i. 140.

chough, a jackdaw, a chattering bird, II. i. 266. See note.

clapp'd, shut fast; V. i. 231.

clear, blameless, unspotted; III. iii. 82.

coil, disturbance, confusion; I. ii. 207.

compassed, brought to pass; III. ii. 66.

complexion, countenance, as indicating character; I. i. 32.

conceive, understand; IV. i. 50.

confederates, forms a league, conspires; I. ii. 111.

constant, firm, self-possessed; I. ii. 207: settled, steady; III. ii. 119.

control, overpower, master; I. ii. 439.

corollary, surplus, extra number; IV. i. 57.

correspondent, obedient, responsive; I. ii. 297.

couch, lie hidden; V. i. 90.

course, course of action, proceeding; II. i. 287.

courses, large lower sails, mainsail and foresail; I. i. 53.

crabs, crab-apples; II. ii. 171.

crack, break, fail; V. i. 2.

K

crisp, curled, rippling; IV. i. 130. Cf. *Henry IV*, I. iii. 106.

dear, affectionate, kindly; I. ii. 141, 179: hard, grievous, severe; II. i. 135; V. i. 146. Probably confused with the preceding meaning, though in origin a different word.

debosh'd, debauched; III. ii. 30.

deck'd, covered; I. ii. 155.

deliver, report; V. i. 313; II. i. 44.

demanded, asked; I. ii. 139.

demi-puppets, tiny dolls; V. i. 36.

dew-lapped, having a fold of loose skin hanging from the throat; III. iii. 45. See note.

diligent, attentive; III. i. 42.

Dis, Pluto; IV. i. 89.

discase, undress, change my attire; V. i. 85.

discharge, execution, performance; II. i. 254: perform; III. i. 22.

discovers, reveals, discloses; V. i. 172, s. d.

dispersedly, from different parts of the stage, in several places; I. ii. 382.

distempered, out of humor, mental equilibrium; disturbed, violent; IV. i. 145.

distinctly, separately; I. ii. 200.

doit, a small coin, half a farthing in value; the merest trifle; II. ii. 33.

dollar, German *Thaler*, Low German *Daler*. Used for the sake of the pun; II. i. 18.

dowle, down, filament of a feather; III. iii. 65.

down, dune, upland; IV. i. 81.

drawn, with swords drawn; II. i. 308; "well drawn," a fine draught; II. ii. 150.

drollery, puppet-show; III. iii. 21. See quotation from Ben Jonson, Introduction, p. xvi.

dry, (1) thirsty, avid; I. ii. 112: (2) severe; IV. i. 260. Cf. *Comedy of Errors*, II. ii. 64.

dulness, sleepiness, stupor; I. ii. 185.

earth'd, buried; II. i. 234.

ebbing, retreating, declining; II. i. 222, 226: " ebbing Neptune," sea tide; V. i. 35.

ecstasy, excitement, frenzy; III. iii. 108.

elements, materials; III. iii. 61.

'em, unaccented form of *hem*, the Old English word for *them*, which is a later word of Scandinavian origin; I. ii. 82, 83; II. ii. 7; III. ii. 3, 130, 131; III. iii. 45; V. i. 265.

engine, instrument of warfare; II. i. 161.

envy, malice; I. ii. 258.

estate, bestow upon; IV. i. 85.

event, outcome, issue, result; I. ii. 117; III. i. 69.

executor, performer; III. i. 13.

extirpate, drive out, expel; I. ii. 125.

eye, slight shade, tinge; II. i. 55.

eyed, looked upon; III. i. 40; V. i. 238.

face, exterior, appearance; see note, I. ii. 104.

fall, cause to fall; II. i. 296; V. i. 64.

fearful, to be feared; I. ii. 468. See note.

feater, more trimly, becomingly; II. i. 273.

featly, deftly, gracefully; I. ii. 380. Cf. *Winter's Tale*, IV. iv. 176.

features, bodily shapes, forms; III. i. 52. Not limited by Shakespeare to the face. Cf. *Richard III*, I. i. 19.

fellowly, sympathetic; V. i. 64.

fellows, companions; I. ii. 416; III, iii. 60; IV. i. 35: equals; II. i. 274; III. i. 84.

few, " in few," in a few words, in brief; I. ii. 144.

filthy-mantled, covered with a filthy scum; IV. i. 182.　Cf. *King Lear*, III. iv. 138.

flatlong, with the side of the blade; II. i. 181.

flesh-fly, a fly that deposits her eggs in flesh; III. i. 63.

float, sea, wave; I. ii. 234.

foil, defeat; "put to the foil," defeated, marred; III. i. 46.

foison, plenty, abundance; IV. i. 110.

forthrights, straight paths; III. iii. 3.

freshes, springs of fresh water; III. ii. 75.

frippery, old-clothes shop; IV. i. 226.

gaberdine, a long, loose outer garment; II. ii. 40, 116.

gilded, made drunk; V. i. 280.　Perhaps an allusion to the *aurum potabile*, the elixir of life.

glasses, hours (by metonymy); I. ii. 240; see note, V. i. 223.

glut, swallow; I. i. 63.

go, walk; III. ii. 22: so, too, "went," II. ii. 63.

grace, blessing, favor; III. i. 75; V. i. 142, 219: kindness; V. i. 70: excellence; III. i. 45: attractiveness; III. iii. 84: mercy, pardon; V. i. 295.

hand, handle; I. i. 25.

heav'd, thrust, expelled; I. ii. 62.

heavily, gloomily; IV. i. 138, stage direction.

heaviness, sadness, sorrow; V. i. 200.

heavy, weary, drowsy, sleepy; II. i. 189, 198: "heavy offer," the offer that brings drowsiness; II. i. 194: hard, severe; III. i. 5.

hest, behest, command; I. ii. 274; III. i. 37; IV. i. 65.

hint, cause, occasion; I. ii. 134; II, i. 3.

his, its; II. i. 120.　See note, II. i. 163.

hollowly, insincerely; III. i. 71.

holp, helped; I. ii. 63.

honey-drops, raindrops sweet as honey; IV. i. 79.

hoodwink, cover up, put out of sight; IV. i. 206.

human, in Elizabethan English not distinguished from *humane;* I. ii. 346.

Hymen, the classical god of marriage; IV. i. 23, 97.

ignorant, causing ignorance; V. i. 67.

ill, evil; I. ii. 457.

inch-meal, inch by inch; II. ii. 3. Cf. *piecemeal.*

increase, produce; IV. i. 110.

Ind, India, the Orient; II. ii. 61.

infect, pollute; V. i. 131. " infect his reason," affect his mind; I. ii. 208. Note "a fever of the mad," line 209.

infest, vex, harass; V. i. 246. Used by Shakespeare only in this passage.

influence, flowing from the star upon him, and thus affecting his destiny; I. ii. 182.

infused, imbued, inspired with; I. ii. 154.

inherit, possess; IV. i. 154; II. ii. 179.

inly, inwardly; V. i. 200.

inquisition, questioning, inquiry; I. ii. 35.

into, unto; I. ii. 100.

invest, put on as a garment; II. i. 226.

it, its, see note, II. i. 163.

Jack, " played the Jack," deceived, played the knave; IV. i. 198.

jerkin, a close-fitting jacket; IV. i. 236.

justify, prove; V. i. 128.

justle, jostle; III. ii. 29; V. i. 158.

key, tuning-key; I. ii. 83. Perhaps with a play upon the keys of office.

kibe, chilblain; II. i. 276.

kindlier, more naturally, more like my kind; V. i. 24.
knot, " in this sad knot," folded sadly thus; I. ii. 224.

lakin, ladykin, little lady, *i.e.*, the Virgin Mary; III. iii. 1.
landed, brought to land; I. ii. 221; V. i. 161.
lass-lorn, forsaken by his lass; IV. i. 68. Cf. " dismissed,"
line 67.
leas, fields, meadows; IV. i. 60.
lieu, " in lieu of," in return for (not in place of); I. ii. 123.
life, lifelikeness, a presentation true to life; III. iii. 86.
like, *adj.*, similar; III. i. 13: *adv.*, alike, equally; III.
iii. 66: *verb*, please; IV. i. 239.
line, see notes, IV. i. 193, 235, 237.
line-grove, grove of lime-trees (lindens); V. i. 10.
list, please; III. ii. 19: pleasest; III. ii. 138.
loathness, disinclination, reluctance, unwillingness; II.
i. 130.
lorded, made a lord, given power in the state; I. ii. 97.

maid, maid-servant; III. i. 84.
main-course, mainsail; I. i. 38.
manage, management, administration; I. ii. 70.
marmoset, a small monkey; II. ii. 174.
marry, to be sure, indeed (a corruption of Mary); III. ii.
46.
massy, heavy, ponderous; III. iii. 67.
matter, something important; II. i. 230.
maze, labyrinth; III. iii. 2; V. i. 242.
mean, lowly, humble; III. i. 4; III. iii. 87; IV. i. 35.
meanders, winding paths, — from the course of the river
Meander in Asia Minor; III. iii. 3.
merchant, merchantman, ship; II. i. 5. Also, in the same
line, with the usual meaning.
merely, absolutely, entirely; I. i. 59.

mettle, disposition, character; II. i. 182.

Milan, lord, ruler, of Milan; V. i. 86, 205.

minion, favorite, darling (French *mignon*); IV. i. 98.

miss, do without; I. ii, 311.

moe, more; II. i. 133; V. i. 234.

momentary, brief, instantaneous; I. ii. 202.

moon-calf, monster, abortion, — because of the supposed influence of the moon; II. ii. 111, 115, 139; III. ii. 24, 25.

mop, grimace; IV. i. 47.

moping, wandering aimlessly in a state of bewilderment; V. i. 240.

mow, grimace (French *moue*); IV. i. 47; III. iii. 82 (stage direction): *verb*, make faces; II. ii. 9.

mudded, covered with mud, buried at the bottom of the sea; III. iii. 102; V. i. 151. Used only in this play.

murrain, a plague; III. ii. 88. Used as an imprecation.

muse, wonder at, marvel at; III. iii. 36. Cf. *Macbeth*, III. iv. 85.

natural, fool, idiot; III. ii. 37: *adj.*, in the realm of nature, as contrasted with that which is supernatural; I. ii. 418; V. i. 157, 227.

nature, disposition, character; I. ii. 93, 359, 497; IV. i. 188: natural feeling, affection; V. i. 76.

neat, cattle; II. ii. 73.

nerves, muscles, sinews; I. ii. 484.

ninny, simpleton, fool; III. ii. 71. Cf. Italian *ninno*, a child.

note, knowledge, information, II. i. 248.

observation, observance, careful attention; III, iii. 87.

occasion, opportunity; II. i. 173, 207.

odd, out of the way, unnoted; I. ii. 223; V. i. 255.

o'erprized, exceeded, surpassed; I. ii. 92.

o'erstunk, stank worse than; IV. i. 184.

of, from; V. i. 142, 194: out of; I. ii. 94, 165: because of; V. i. 230: denoting the material constituting a thing; I. ii. 101, 374, 397; II. ii. 127; III. i. 9, 48; III. ii. 79: about; I. ii. 119, 433: for; II. i. 2: most of; I. ii. 69: belonging to; I. i. 24; II. i. 82.

off and on, to and fro, back and forth; III. ii. 17.

old, well-known, familiar; or, perhaps, characteristic of old age; I. ii. 369. Cf. III. iii. 2, and IV. i. 261.

omit, ignore, neglect; I. ii. 183.

on, of; I. ii. 87, 456; IV. i. 157; V. i. 162: upon; V. i. 4.

or, before; see note, I. ii. 11; V. i. 103.

out, fully, completely; I. ii. 41; IV. i. 101: loudly; I. ii. 133: at an end, finished; I. ii. 246; III. ii. 1.

over-blown, blown over, passed by; II. ii. 114.

over-topping, rising too high, out-stripping; I. ii. 81.

owes, owns, possesses; I. ii. 407, 454; III. i. 45.

own, master of himself; V. i. 213.

pains, tasks; I. ii. 242.

pard, panther, leopard; IV. i. 262.

pass of pate, sally of wit; IV. i. 244. A *pass* is a thrust in fencing.

passion, grief, sorrow; I. ii. 392: strong emotion; IV. i. 143; V. i. 24. Cf. *Acts* xiv. 15.

patch, fool, one attired like a professional jester, in motley; III. ii. 71. Cf. " pied ninny."

pate, head; IV. i. 244.

paunch, stab in the paunch, belly; III. ii. 98.

perdition, loss; I. ii. 30: destruction; III. iii. 77. For both uses cf. *Othello*, II. ii. 3 and III. iii. 90.

pertly, briskly, promptly; IV. i. 58.

piece, a perfect specimen, a model, a masterpiece; I. ii. 56.

pied, parti-colored; III. ii. 71. See " patch " above.

pierces, affects, touches, moves deeply; Epilogue, 17.

pike, a sharp-pointed weapon, somewhat like a spear, used for thrusting, not for hurling; II. i. 161.

pioned, see note, IV. i. 64.

plantation, colonization; II. i. 143. Cf. "Providence Plantations" and Bacon's Essay, "Of Plantations." Antonio and Sebastian take the word in its ordinary meaning, — "planting."

point, sting; V. i. 138: particular; I. ii. 501: "to point," to the smallest detail, exactly; I. ii. 194.

pole-clipt, referring to a vineyard in which the poles are clipt, embraced, twined about by the vines; IV. i. 68.

Poor-John, hake, salted and dried; II. ii. 28.

premises, terms, conditions previously made; I. ii. 123.

presently, immediately, instantly; I. ii. 125; IV. i. 42; V. I. 101.

prevent, forestall, anticipate, and thus hinder; I. ii. 350.

prithee, [I] pray thee; I. ii. 246 *et passim*.

profess, declare, avow; III. i. 69; to make one's business or profession; II. i. 236.

proper, own; III. iii. 60: fine, handsome; II. ii. 63.

provision, care, foresight; I. ii. 28.

purchased, won, gained, acquired; IV. i. 14.

putter-out, see note, III. iii. 48.

quaint, fine, dainty; I. ii. 317.

quality, nature, character; I. ii. 337; II. i. 200: skill, capacity; I. ii. 193.

quick, living; "quick freshes," springs of fresh water; III. ii. 75.

quickens, gives life to; III. i. 6.

rabble, crowd; IV. i. 37. Not necessarily used in a contemptuous way. Cf. "meaner fellows," line 35.

race, inherited nature; I. ii. 358.

rack, thin, drifting cloud in the upper air; IV. i. 156. See note.

rate, judgment, estimation; II. i. 109: "popular rate," estimation of the people; I. ii. 92.

razorable, fit to be shaved; II. i. 250.

rear, raise; II. i. 295.

reeling ripe, drunk enough to be on the point of reeling; V. i. 279.

remember, be mindful. consider; I. i. 20: remind; I. ii. 243: mention; I. ii. 405.

remembrance, memory, faculty of remembering; II, i. 232.

remorse, pity, compassion; V. i. 76.

renown, report, praise; V. i. 193.

required, asked for; V. i. 51.

requit, requited; III. iii. 71. Cf. *betid*, I. ii. 31.

resolve, inform, put in possession of; V. i. 248.

rid, destroy; I. ii. 364.

rifted, cleft, split; V. i. 45.

rounded, rounded out, completed; or, emcompassed, has its beginning and ending in; IV. i. 158.

royalties, rights and prerogatives of a sovereign; I. ii. 110.

sack, a name for white wines from Southern Europe; II. ii. 125; III. ii. 15, 32, 88. Formerly written "seck": cf. Spanish *seco*, French *sec*.

sanctimonious, holy, sacred; IV. i. 16.

sans, without; I. ii. 97.

scamels, meaning uncertain, see note; II. ii. 176.

scandal'd, scandalous, disgraceful; IV. i. 90.

sea-change, a change caused by the sea; I. ii. 400.

sedg'd, made of sedge, flags, rushes; IV. i. 129.

sensible, sensitive; II. i. 174.

sets off, see note, III. i. 2.

setting, aspect, fixed look; II. i. 229.

shroud, take shelter; II. ii. 43.

signories, principalities; I. ii. 71.

siege, stool, excrement; II. i. 110.

single, weak, feeble, — also solitary, alone; I. ii. 432:
alone, in private; V. i. 248.

sirrah, used in addressing inferiors; V. i. 287, 291.

skilless, ignorant; III. i. 53.

solemn, stately, venerable; IV. i. 153: sad, melancholy;
III. iii. 17, stage direction; V. i. 40, 58.

something, somewhat; I. ii. 414.

sooth, truth; II. ii. 150.

sorcerer, magician; III. ii. 49.

sorcery, magic, III. ii. 60.

sot, fool, dullard (French *sot*); III. ii. 101.

sour-eyed, with sullen look; IV. i. 20.

speak, proclaim; II. i. 8, 207.

spiriting, duties as a spirit; I. ii. 298.

sprites, spirits; I. ii. 381; II. ii. 120.

spurs, roots; V. i. 47.

stain'd, disfigured, I. ii. 414.

stale, decoy, bait; IV. i. 187.

standard, standard-bearer, with quibble on "stand";
III. ii. 18.

state, rank; by metonymy, duties of state; I. ii. 76.

steaded, helped, been of service; I. ii. 165.

still, always, ever; IV. i. 108; V. i. 214. See also I.
ii. 229; III. iii. 64.

stock-fish, dried cod; "make a stock-fish of thee," give
thee a beating, as dried cod was beaten before it was
boiled; III. ii. 79.

stomach, appetite; III. iii. 41: inclination; II. i. 107:
courage; I. ii. 157.

stover, fodder; IV. i. 63.

strange, unfamiliar, rare, unusual; II. i. 112; II. ii. 28, 32; III. iii. 87; V. i. 228.

strangely, rarely, uncommonly; IV. i. 7.

sty, keep as in a sty; I. ii. 342.

substitution, deputyship; " out o' the substitution," in consequence of being my deputy; I. ii. 103.

subtleties, deceptions, illusions; V. i. 124. See note.

succession, inheriting of property; II. i. 151.

suggestion, prompting to evil, temptation; II. i. 288; IV. i. 26.

sustaining, upholding, bearing up; or enduring the effect of salt water; I. ii. 218. Cf. *Hamlet*, IV. vii. 176, 177.

swabber, one who washes or swabs the deck; II. ii. 48.

tabor, a small drum; III. ii. 133, s. d.; IV. i. 175.

taborer, a player on the tabor; III. ii. 160.

tackle, ropes, rigging; I. ii. 147.

tang, something that leaves a sting behind it, perhaps here associated with " tang," a sharp sound; II. ii. 52.

teen, trouble, anxiety; I. ii. 64.

tell, count (the strokes of the clock); II. i. 15, 289.

temperance, climate, temperature; II. i. 42. As a proper name (with a pun), line 43.

temperate, chaste; IV. i. 132. Cf. line 66.

temporal, belonging to the world, — as contrasted with his library; I. ii. 110.

tend, attend to, listen to; I. i. 7: serve, wait on; I. ii. 47.

tender, regard; II. i. 270: offer; IV. i. 5.

thatch'd, covered; IV. i. 63.

third, see note, IV. i. 3.

thou'rt, thou wert; I. ii. 366.

throes, causes pain; II. i. 231.

throughly, thoroughly; III. iii. 14. Cf. *Psalm* li. 2.

tilth, tillage, cultivation; II. i. 152.

to, for; I. ii. 129; II. i. 75; III. iii. 54: compared to; I. ii. 480, 481; II. i. 178.

trash, see note, I. ii. 81.

trenchering, a "trencher" was a wooden plate or platter; perhaps formed by the drunken Caliban, who should have said "trencher," but who felt the impulse to rime with "firing," etc.; II. ii. 187.

trice, "on a trice," in a moment; V. i. 238.

tricksy, sportive; or, full of devices, resourceful; V. i. 226.

trifle, phantom; or, trick of magic; V. i. 112.

troll, sing; III. ii. 126.

trumpery, deceptive trifles (cf. French *tromperie*); IV. i. 186.

try, "bring her to try," bring her close to the wind; I. i. 38.

twangling, vibrating, sounding; III. ii. 146.

twilled, see note, IV. i. 64.

twink, twinkling; IV. i. 43.

unback'd, never ridden, untamed; IV. i. 176.

undergo, suffer, submit to; III. i. 27: see also III. i. 3; I. ii. 157.

uneasy, difficult; I. ii. 451.

unmitigable, implacable; I. ii. 276.

unstanched, leaky, used figuratively; I. i. 51.

upon, because of, in obedience to; III. i. 11.

up-staring, standing on end; I. ii. 213. Cf. *Julius Cæsar*, IV. iii. 280.

urchins, goblins (original meaning hedgehogs); I. ii. 326. See note.

urchin-shows, apparitions of goblins; II. ii. 5.

use, are accustomed; II. i. 175: practise; III. iii. 16: treat; V. i. 72; I. ii. 345.

vanity, illusion; IV. i. 41.

varlets, knaves, rascals; IV. i. 170.

vast, waste or desolate period (of night); I. ii. 327. Cf. *Hamlet,* I. ii. 198.

vetches, tares, forage plants; IV. i. 61.

vex'd, troubled, distressed; IV. i. 158.

virgin knot, a reference to the zone or girdle that was worn by maidens in classical times; IV. i. 15.

visitation, visiting, affliction by the plague; III. i. 32.

vouch'd, asserted, warranted; II. i. 60.

waist, in the waist, amidships; I. ii. 197.

wallets of flesh, see note on III. iii. 46.

waste, spend; V. i. 302. Cf. *Merchant of Venice,* III. iv. 12.

ways, "come your ways," come along; II. ii. 85.

weather, storm; I. i. 40; II. ii. 19.

weather-fends, shelters, protects from the weather; V. i. 10.

welkin, sky; I. ii. 4.

wench, sometimes used as a familiar term of endearment, as in I. ii. 139, 412, 479.

went, walked; II. ii. 63. Cf. *go,* III. ii. 22.

wezand, windpipe; III. ii. 99.

whe'er, contraction for whether; V. i. 111.

when, which time; V. i. 250: an exclamation of impatience; I. ii. 316. Cf. *Julius Cæsar,* II. i. 5.

whist, hushed, silenced; or into silence; see note, I. ii. 379.

wide-chapp'd, wide-mouthed, open-mouthed; I. i. 60.

wink, an instant; II. i. 242: "the perpetual wink," the sleep of death; II. i. 285.

wink'st, closest the eyes; II. i. 216.

wisest, "after the wisest," in the wisest way; II. ii. 77.

withal, therewith, with it; III. i. 93; III. ii. 105.

wond'red, wonder-working, full of wonder; IV. i. 123.

worm, an expression of pity; III. i. 31.

wrangle, dispute, quarrel; V. i. 174.
wrong, harm, injury; I. ii. 151; see note, I. ii. 443.

yare, ready, active, brisk, I. i. 37; V. i. 224.
yarely, briskly, nimbly; I. i. 4.
yond, yonder; II. ii. 20, 21, 24; I. ii. 409.

Printed in the United States of America.

THE following pages contain advertisements of other volumes of The Tudor Shakespeare, Macmillan's Pocket Series of English Classics, and important Shakespeariana.

The Tudor Shakespeare Series

An unexpurgated edition for library and general use. Under the general editorship of Professor WILLIAM ALLEN NEILSON of Harvard University and Professor ASHLEY HORACE THORNDIKE of Columbia University. Notes, glossaries, and introductions scholarly and unobtrusive.

Pocket Classics Edition, cloth, 25 cents each

Superior Cloth Edition, 35 cents each

De Luxe Edition, leather, 55 cents each

All's Well That Ends Well.
(Lowes.)

Antony and Cleopatra. (Benedict.)

As You Like It. (Shackford.)

Comedy of Errors. (Padelford.)

Coriolanus. (Sherman.)

Cymbeline. (Howe.)

Hamlet. (Baker.)

Henry IV, Part I. (Chandler.)

Henry IV, Part II. (Hanscom.)

Henry V. (Mott.)

Henry VI, Part I. (Pound.)

Henry VI, Part II. (Barnwell.)

Henry VI, Part III. (Law.)

Henry VIII. (Dunlap.)

Julius Cæsar. (Lovett.)

King John. (Belden.)

King Lear. (Gildersleeve.)

Love's Labour's Lost. (Royster.)

Macbeth. (Brown.)

Measure for Measure. (Morris.)

Merchant of Venice. (Ayres.)

Merry Wives of Windsor. (Emery.)

Midsummer-Night's Dream.
(Cunliffe.)

Much Ado About Nothing.
(Lawrence.)

Othello. (Parrott.)

Pericles. (Smith.)

Richard II. (Craige.)

Richard III. (Churchill.)

Romeo and Juliet. (Neilson and Thorndike.)

The Sonnets. (Alden.)

Taming of the Shrew. (Tupper.)

The Tempest. (Greene.)

Timon of Athens. (Fletcher.)

Titus Andronicus. (Stoll.)

Troilus and Cressida. (Tatlock.)

Twelfth Night. (Hart.)

Two Gentlemen of Verona.
(Sampson.)

Venus and Adonis, and Lucrece.
(Brown.)

Winter's Tale. (Wylie.)

Facts about Shakespeare.
(Neilson and Thorndike.)

MACMILLAN'S
Pocket American and English Classics

Cloth. Uniform in size and binding, 25 cents each

---

1. This well-known Series includes over 150 volumes suitable for class-room, reading circle, or library.

2. Edited in most cases by teachers experienced in teaching English in secondary schools, and in all cases by people familiar with high school needs, they are ideal books for the high school course.

3. Among the titles in the Series will be found the masterpieces of the language.

4. The text of each classic has received special attention, and the editing is marked by sound scholarship and judgment. The notes are suggestive and helpful.

5. The little books are well printed on good paper; they are firmly bound in serviceable gray cloth; and in every sense of the word the workmanship of the Series is excellent.

Addison's Sir Roger de Coverley. (Gray.)
Andersen's Danish Fairy Tales and Legends. (Brooks.)
Arabian Nights. (Johnson.)
Arnold's Sohrab and Rustum, and other Poems. (Castleman.)
Austen's Pride and Prejudice. (Heermans.)
Austen's Sense and Sensibility. (Miller.) *Preparing.*
Bacon's Essays. (Clarke.)
Baker's Out of the Northland. (E. K. Baker.)
Blackmore's Lorna Doone. (Barbour.)
Selections from Boswell's Life of Johnson. (Watson.) *Preparing.*
Mrs. Browning's Poems. Selection. (Hersey.)
Browning's Shorter Poems. (F. T. Baker.)
Bryant's Thanatopsis, Sella, and other Poems. (Castleman.)
Bulwer Lytton's Last Days of Pompeii. (Castleman.)
Bunyan's Pilgrim's Progress. (Moffatt.)
Burke's Speech on Conciliation with America. (Newsom.)
Burns's Poems. (Buck.)
Byron's Childe Harold's Pilgrimage. (George.)

Byron's Shorter Poems. (Bowles.)

Carlyle's Essay on Burns. (Gore.)

Carlyle's Heroes and Hero Worship. (Marble.)

Carroll's Alice in Wonderland. (McMurry.)

Chaucer's Prologue. The Knight's Tale; The Nun's Priest's Tale. (Ingraham.)

Church's The Story of the Iliad.

Church's The Story of the Odyssey.

Coleridge's The Ancient Mariner, Kubla Khan, and Christabel. (Huntington.)

Collection of Short Stories. (Pittinger.) *Preparing.*

Cooper's Last of the Mohicans. (Wickes.)

Cooper's The Deerslayer.

Cooper's The Spy. (Thurber.)

Dana's Two Years before the Mast. (Keyes.)

Defoe's Robinson Crusoe. Part I. (Gaston.)

Defoe's The Life and Adventures of Robinson Crusoe. Abridged. (Johnson.)

De Quincey's Confessions of an English Opium-Eater. (Beatty.)

De Quincey's Essays: Joan of Arc, The English Mail Coach, and The Spanish Military Nun. (Newman.)

Dickens's Christmas Carol. (Sawin and Thomas.)

Dickens's David Copperfield. 2 volumes. (Fairley.)

Dickens's Tale of Two Cities. (Buehler and Mason.)

Dryden's Palamon and Arcite. (Chubb.)

Early American Orations, 1760–1824. (Heller.)

Jonathan Edwards's Sermons. Selections. (Gardiner.)

Eliot's Silas Marner. (Gulick.)

Eliot's Mill on the Floss. (Ausherman.) *Preparing.*

Emerson's Earlier Poems. (Gallagher.)

Emerson's Essays. (Holmes.)

Emerson's Representative Men. (Buck.)

English Narrative Poems. (Fuess and Sanborn.)

Epoch-making Papers in United States History. (Brown.)

Franklin's Autobiography.

Mrs. Gaskell's Cranford. (Sampson.)

Goldsmith's The Deserted Village, and other Poems. (Whiteford.)

Goldsmith's Vicar of Wakefield. (Boynton.)

Gray's Elegy in a Country Church-yard and Cowper's John Gilpin's Ride. (Castleman.)

Grimm's Fairy Tales. (Fassett.)

Hale's The Man without a Country. (Tucker.)

Hawthorne's Grandfather's Chair. (Kingsley.)

Hawthorne's House of the Seven Gables. (Furst.)

Hawthorne's Mosses from an Old Manse. (Burbank.)

Hawthorne's Tanglewood Tales. (Beggs.)

Hawthorne's Twice-told Tales. (Gaston.)

Hawthorne's Wonder Book. (Wolfe.)

Holmes's Poems. Selections. (Castleman.)

Holmes's Autocrat of the Breakfast Table. (Rounds.) *Preparing.*

Homer's Iliad. Lang, Leaf, and Meyers Trans.

Homer's Iliad. Pope Trans. Complete. (Rhodes.)

Homer's Odyssey. Butcher and Lang Trans. (Carpenter.)

Homer's Odyssey. Pope Trans. Complete. (Shumway.)

Hughes's Tom Brown's School Days. (Thomas.)

Huxley's Selected Essays and Addresses. (Buck.)

Irving's Alhambra. (Hitchcock.)

Irving's Knickerbocker History of New York. (Greenlaw.)

Irving's Life of Goldsmith. (Blakely.)

Irving's Sketch Book.

Irving's Tale of a Traveler. (Chase.)

Keary's The Heroes of Asgard. (Morss.)

Thomas a Kempis's The Imitation of Christ. (Brother Leo.)

Kingsley's The Heroes, or Greek Fairy Tales. (McMurry.)

Lamb's Essays of Elia. (Robins.)

Lamb's Tales from Shakespeare. (Ainger.)

Selections from Lincoln's Addresses. (Chubb.)

Selections from Lockhart's Life of Scott. (Reid.) *Preparing.*

Longfellow's Courtship of Miles Standish. (Lewis.)

Longfellow's Courtship of Miles Standish, and Minor Poems. (Howe.)

Longfellow's Evangeline. (Semple.)

Longfellow's The Song of Hiawatha. (Fleming.)

Longfellow's Tales of a Wayside Inn. (Castleman.)

Lowell's The Vision of Sir Launfal. (Bates.)

Macaulay's Essay on Addison. (French.)

Macaulay's Essay on Clive. (Pearce.)

Macaulay's Essay on Milton. (French.)
Macaulay's Essay on Warren Hastings. (Frick.)
Macaulay's Lays of Ancient Rome, and other Poems. (F. T. Baker.)
Macaulay's Life of Johnson. (Schuyler.)
Malory's Morte d'Arthur. (Swiggett.)
Memorable Passages from the Bible. Authorized Version. (Scott.)
Milton's Comus, Lycidas, and other Poems, and Matthew Arnold's
    Address on Milton. (Allen.)
Milton's Paradise Lost. Books I and II. (Crane.)
Old English Ballads. (Armes.)
Old Testament Selections. (Scott.)
Palgrave's Golden Treasury of Songs and Lyrics.
Parkman's The Oregon Trail. (Douglas.)
Plutarch's Lives of Cæsar, Brutus, and Antony. (Brier.)
Poe's Poems. (Kent.)
Poe's Prose Tales. Selections.
Poems Narrative and Lyrical. (St. John.)
Pope's Iliad. (Rhodes.)
Pope's Iliad : Books I, VI, XXII, XXIV. (Smyth.)
Pope's Odyssey. (E. S. and W. Shumway.)
Pope's Rape of the Lock. (King.)
Christina Rossetti's Poems. Selections. (Burke.)
Ruskin's Crown of Wild Olive, and Queen of the Air. (Melton.)
Ruskin's Sesame and Lilies, and The King of the Golden River.
    (Bates.)
Scott's Ivanhoe. (Hitchcock.)
Scott's Kenilworth. (Castleman.)
Scott's Lady of the Lake. (Packard.)
Scott's Lay of the Last Minstrel. (Bowles.)
Scott's Marmion. (Aiton.)
Scott's Quentin Durward. (Eno.)
Scott's Talisman. (Treudley.)
Select Orations. (Hall.)
Selected Poems for Required Reading in Secondary Schools. (Boyn-
    ton.)
Selections for Oral English. (Fuess.) *Preparing.*
Shakespeare's As You Like It. (Gaston.)
Shakespeare's Hamlet. (Sherman.)

5

Shakespeare's King Henry V. (Bowles.)
Shakespeare's Julius Cæsar. (G. W. and L. G. Hufford.)
Shakespeare's King Richard II. (Moffatt.)
Shakespeare's King Lear. (Buck.)
Shakespeare's Macbeth. (French.)
Shakespeare's Merchant of Venice. (Underwood.)
Shakespeare's Midsummer-Night's Dream. (Noyes.)
Shakespeare's The Tempest. (Newsom.)
Shakespeare's Twelfth Night. (Morton.)
Shelley and Keats. Selections. (Newsom.)
Sheridan's The Rivals, and The School for Scandal. (Howe.)
Southern Orators. (McConnell.)
Southern Poets. Selections. (Weber.)
Spenser's Faerie Queene, Book I. (Wauchope.)
Stevenson's Kidnapped. (Brown.)
Stevenson's Master of Ballantrae. (White.)
Stevenson's Treasure Island. (Vance.)
Swift's Gulliver's Travels. (Johnson.)
Tennyson's Idylls of the King. (French.)
Stevenson's Travels with a Donkey, and An Inland Voyage. (Cross.)
Tennyson's Princess. (Farrand.)
Tennyson's Shorter Poems. (Nutter.)
Thackeray's English Humorists. (Castleman.)
Thackeray's Henry Esmond. (Henneman.)
Thoreau's Walden. (Rees.)
The Æneid of Virgil. Conington Trans. (Shumway.)
Selections from Trevelyan's Life of Macaulay. (Barley.) *Preparing*.
Washington's Farewell Address, and Webster's Bunker Hill Orations.
    (Peck.)
Whittier's Snow-bound, and other Poems. (Bouton.)
John Woolman's Journal.
Wordsworth's Shorter Poems. (Fulton.)

THE MACMILLAN COMPANY

Publishers   64-66 Fifth Avenue   New York

The Development of Shakespeare as a Dramatist

By GEORGE PIERCE BAKER, Professor of English in Harvard University. *Cloth, crown 8vo, $2.00*   *by mail, $2.15*

The book endeavors to fill a gap in the discussions of Shakespeare's art by distinguishing his debt as a dramatic writer to his predecessors or contemporaries, indicating his contribution to each of the varied forms, chronicle play, farce, melodrama, comedy of manners, high comedy, and tragedy. Professor Baker has made clear the interesting progress of the dramatist toward the mastery of his art, and has illustrated the work with views of London and of the life of the theatre in Shakespeare's day.

What is Shakespeare?

An Introduction to the Great Plays

By L. A. SHERMAN, Professor of English Literature in the University of Nebraska. *Cloth, large 12mo, xii + 414 pp., $1.00*

Short Sketches of Shakespeare's Plots

By CYRIL RANSOME, Professor of Modern Literature and History in the Yorkshire College of the Victoria University.
Cloth, 12mo, viii + 299 pp., $1.00

Shakespeare's Heroines

By ANNA JAMESON. With twenty-six portraits of famous players in character   *Cloth, 8vo, 341 pp., $2.00*
The same without the illustrations. Bohn Library. *$1.00*

Shakespeare in Tale and Verse

By LOIS G. HUFFORD.   *Cloth, 12mo, ix + 445 pp., $1.00*
The same. Standard School Library.   *$.50*

Lamb's Tales from Shakespeare

By CHARLES and MARY LAMB. Illustrated by Byam Shaw. *$2.50*
The same. Eversley Series. *$1.50.* The same. Bohn Library Edition. *$1.00*
Pocket Classics Edition. Edited by Canon Ainger. *$.25.* English Classics Edition. *$.40.* Standard School Library. *$.50*
Golden Treasury Series. *$1.00.*

Characters of Shakespeare's Plays

By WILLIAM HAZLITT.   *Cloth, $1.50*

Shakespeare's Songs and Sonnets

Edited by FRANCIS T. PALGRAVE. Golden Treasury Series. *$1.00*

Shakespearean Tragedy *Second Edition*

Lectures on Hamlet, Othello, King Lear, and Macbeth

By A. C. BRADLEY, LL.D., Litt.D., Professor of Poetry in the University of Oxford.

Cloth, 8vo, xii + 498 pages, $3.25 *by mail, $3.40*

The Times, London: —

"Nothing has been written for many years that has done so much as these lectures will do to advance the underst ding and the appreciation of the greatest things in Shakespeare's greatest plays. . . . One may well doubt whether in the whole field of English literary criticism anything has been written in the last twenty years more luminous, more masterly, more penetrating to the very centre of its subject."

Shakespeare: *A Critical Study*

By GEORGE BRANDES, Author of "Main Currents of Nineteenth Century Literature," etc. *Cloth, 8vo, 690 pages and index, $2.60*

The Athenæum, London: —

"On these volumes as a whole we can bestow hearty praise and commendation. No other single work on Shakespeare includes so much, and so much that is valuable. Dr. Brandes is a good, a first-rate 'all-round man.' There is no side of his subject which he neglects. He is both an antiquary and a critic, interested in the smallest details of biography, and also taking broad and comprehensive views of Shakespeare's thought and style. His book is in its way encyclopædic, and we venture to say that there are few people — few scholars — who would not find themselves the better informed and the wiser for its perusal. He has equipped himself for his task by wide study and research; and on all the materials he has amassed he has brought to bear a judgment well balanced and vigorous, and a mind liberal and independent. It is many years since there has been any contribution to Shakespearean literature of such importance as this. These two volumes are of solid worth, and deserve a place in every Shakespearean student's library."

Eighteenth Century Essays on Shakespeare

Edited by D. NICHOL SMITH. *Cloth, $3.00*

From the Editor's Preface: —

"It is at least eighty years since most of these Essays were reprinted. Rowe's Account of Shakespeare is given in its original and complete form for the first time, it is believed, since 1714. . . . Dennis's Essay has not appeared since the author republished it in 1721. . . . The Nine Essays or Prefaces here reprinted may claim to represent the chief phases of Shakespearean study from the days of Dryden to those of Coleridge. The Introduction has been planned to show the main lines in the development of Shakespeare's reputation, and to prove that the new criticism, which is said to begin with Coleridge, takes its rise as early as the third quarter of the eighteenth century."